THE EAGLE HAS LANDED

The Story of Apollo 11

JEFFREY K. SMITH

ISBN-10: 1480127744
EAN-13: 978-1480127746
Library of Congress Control Number: 2012920319
New Frontier Publications, North Charleston, South Carolina

NOTE TO READERS

More than once, I have been questioned about the absence of footnotes or endnotes in my non-fiction books. Simply answered—it is a matter of style. While recounting the lives and times of historical figures, I have chosen to present their stories in narrative format. It is my goal to *bring history alive,* akin to a fast-paced novel. The chronology and accuracy of the events in this book and my other works of non-fiction are substantiated by extensive research, with the sources listed in the bibliography. Ultimately, I hope readers will understand that fact is often stranger and more compelling than fiction.

PROLOGUE

It all began with a blinking light racing across the nighttime skies. A silver-colored satellite, the size of a basketball and weighing 184 pounds, was orbiting the Earth once every 96 minutes at the unheard of speed of 17,000 miles per hour. Christened *Sputnik* by its Russian designers, the world's first orbiting satellite was launched on October 4, 1957.

Soviet Premiere Nikita Khrushchev gloated: "People of the whole world are pointing to the satellite. They are saying the United States has been beaten."

In a decade dominated by McCarthyism and the exaggerated "Red Scare," civilian and military leaders were suddenly pressured to unveil America's own plans for space exploration. Thus began the *Space Race.*

Early on, the contest was decidedly in favor of the Soviet Union, as the U.S. struggled to catch up with their Communist rivals. Eventually, the tide turned, and America overtook its Cold War foe, culminating in what many still consider the greatest technological feat of the 20th century.

On July 20, 1969, as a worldwide television audience of 500 million watched, Neil Armstrong became the first human to set foot on the Moon. Nearly a half-century later, Armstrong's words still resonate: "That's one small step for man, one giant leap for mankind."

Barely a decade after entering the Space Race, the United States had achieved the unthinkable. The combined efforts of 400,000 individuals led to the successful design, development, and implementation of the *Apollo 11* lunar landing mission.

While the Space Race is commonly remembered as a time of innovation and technological advances, powerful, yet often overlooked forces were also at play. Politics and money were among the prime catalysts of space exploration. Opportunists exploited the emotions of fellow Americans, many of whom genuinely feared nuclear annihilation by the Soviet Union. While history was being made and new heroes were discovered, the aerospace industry reaped enormous profits and political careers blossomed.

The Eagle Has Landed: The Story of Apollo 11 chronicles the triumphs and tragedies of America's quest to land a man on the Moon, beginning with the stories of the visionaries who made space exploration a reality. It is a remarkable story of political gamesmanship, innovation, perseverance, and courage.

CHAPTER 1

Yes, to the Moon

A t a quarter past four on the morning on Wednesday, July 16, 1969, the *Apollo 11* astronauts received their wake-up calls. After final physical examinations by NASA flight surgeons, Neil Armstrong, Buzz Aldrin, and Michael Collins had a final sit-down meeting with the Director of Flight Crew Operations, Donald "Deke" Slayton.

Over a breakfast of steak, scrambled eggs, toast, orange juice, and coffee, the four men reviewed the events of the coming day. Across the room, artist Paul Calle sketched the astronauts while they ate; the first of many lasting visual images from that historic day.

After breakfast, the trio entered the *suit room* to don their launch garb. The *Apollo 11* crew had already spent two weeks in virtual quarantine to minimize the risk of exposure to infectious diseases prior to their space flight. After medical bio-sensory leads were attached to their torso and limbs, the three men slipped into their white nylon jump suits. With the assistance of experienced technicians, the astronauts then squeezed inside their pressurized spacesuits. Finally, their helmets and visors were snapped shut, completely isolating them from the outside world.

At 5:30 a.m., the astronauts exited the Kennedy Center for Manned Spacecraft Operations, and boarded a van for transport to launch pad 39A. Clutching their portable ventilators in one hand, Armstrong, Aldrin, and Collins used the other to wave at the reporters gathered outside the building.

While the majority of the world viewed them as courageous explorers, the astronauts were indeed very human. Neil Armstrong carried a comb and a package of *Lifesavers* in his pocket, while Buzz Aldrin pocketed pictures of his three children.

At Cape Canaveral, Florida, over a half-million people had gathered to witness the launch of *Apollo 11*. The neighboring highways were hopelessly clogged, resulting in a 10-mile-long traffic jam. Fires smoldered along the beaches and in the surrounding wooded areas, where eager space enthusiasts had camped all night. Thousands of boats were anchored on the nearby Indian and Banana Rivers, positioned to capture a bird's eye view of the historic launch. Worldwide, 25 million viewers huddled around their television sets.

NASA had invited over 20,000 VIPs to view the launch, including some 250 members of Congress, half of the states' Governors, former President Lyndon B. Johnson, and the current Vice-President, Spiro T. Agnew. Jack Benny and Johnny Carson were among the notables representing the entertainment world. Over 3,000 journalists, representing 56 countries, had been issued press passes.

A viewing area had been established three miles from the launch pad, with bleachers, portable toilets, water tanks, and refreshment stands. Even though it was still early morning, the Florida heat and humidity were already extracting a heavy toll from the assembled guests. Among the most anxious of the observers were the astronaut's wives, all of whom had traveled from their homes in Houston to Cape Canaveral to witness the launch. Neil Armstrong's wife, Janet, stared at the monstrous launch rocket from a yacht anchored on the Banana River.

During the 1960s, demonstrations had become commonplace, and on this sweltering summer morning, a group of 150 protesters

2

led by civil rights leader, Reverend Ralph Abernathy, gathered within sight of the launch pad. As representatives of the *Poor Peoples' Campaign*, Abernathy and his followers loudly decried the government's "foolish waste of money that could be used to feed the poor."

At daybreak, Wernher von Braun, the German-born rocket scientist who had supervised the design of the *Saturn V* rocket that would propel the *Apollo 11* crew into space, kissed his wife goodbye, before leaving the Cocoa Beach *Holiday Inn*.

"Pray," he implored.

"Bye and good luck," she replied.

To bypass the snarled roadways, von Braun was flown by helicopter to nearby Cape Canaveral. During the final countdown, the man known as the "Father of the American space program," bowed his head and recited the Lord's Prayer.

When the astronauts arrived at the launch pad, the 363-feet-tall *Saturn V* rocket towered above, attached by umbilical lines to a steel support tower. After briefly glancing skyward, Armstrong, Aldrin, and Collins glided up the elevator to the space capsule perched atop the mammoth rocket.

Three-quarters of the way up, the elevator halted, and Buzz Aldrin stepped onto a platform and waited, while his crewmates were carried the rest of the way to the top. Standing alone, isolated from the outside world in his pressurized spacesuit, Aldrin stared at the rising sun over the Atlantic Ocean. The veteran astronaut, who had spent thousands of hours training for this historic mission, prepared to be hurtled into space for the second time in five years.

Inside the capsule boarding area, known as the *white room*, Armstrong and Collins entered the *Apollo* capsule first. Aldrin, who had temporarily waited below to ease overcrowding, was the last to arrive and board the tiny command service module (CSM), which would serve as the astronauts' home for the next eight days.

Fred Haise, the back-up lunar module pilot, had just exited the CSM, christened *Columbia*, having completed a checklist of 417 pre-flight tests. Haise wished his fellow astronauts good luck, before taking the elevator down.

The crew squeezed into their *couches*—NASA terminology for cockpit seats. Mission commander Armstrong sat on the left, with Collins on the right, and Aldrin positioned in the middle. Before closing the capsule hatch, launch pad lead technician Guenter Wendt presented Armstrong with a going away present—a crescent moon carved out of Styrofoam and covered with tin foil. In the distant horizon, invisible to the naked eye, a thin sliver of moon, a quarter of a million miles away, kept watch over Cape Canaveral.

Once the launch pad technicians sealed the capsule hatch, Armstrong, Aldrin, and Collins would have no face-to-face contact with other humans for more than a week. Adding to the drama, the *Apollo 11* crew was keenly aware that any one of a number of potentially fatal mishaps could leave them stranded in space forever.

Command module pilot Michael Collins silently reflected on his forthcoming role in history: "Here I am, a white male, age 30, height 5-feet 11-inches, weight 165 pounds, salary $17,000 per annum; resident of a Texas suburb, with a black spot on my roses; state of mind unsettled, about to be shot off the to Moon—yes, to the Moon."

CHAPTER 2
Luna

Mankind's fascination with the Moon dates back many centuries. Celestial observers have long been intrigued by its cyclical phases and captivated by the wonderment of infrequent solar and lunar eclipses. For generations, the origin and composition of this celestial body remained a mystery. The Romans named it *Luna,* while the Greeks called it *Selene* or *Artemis.* In the developing Western civilizations, it was simply known as the *Moon*—a word of Germanic origin.

In 1609, Italian astronomer, physicist, and mathematician Galileo Galilei began studying the Moon closely, utilizing the telescope; an instrument invented a year earlier in the Netherlands. Using his "spyglass" and artistic skills, Galileo drew detailed sketches in his publication, *Siderus Nuncius.* Originally thought to be smooth sphere, Galileo's illustrations revealed the true topography of the lunar surface—craters surrounded by rugged mountains.

A year later, German mathematician and astronomer John Kepler extended Galileo's vision to foretell of space exploration: "Let us create vessels and sails adjusted to the heavenly ether, and there will be plenty of people unafraid of the empty wastes. In the meantime, we shall prepare, for the brave sky travelers, maps of celestial bodies. I shall do it for the Moon, you Galileo, for Jupiter."

The upper echelons of the Roman Catholic Church soon branded Galileo as a heretic for challenging the Aristotelian/ Ptolemaic Theory that the Sun, Moon, and planets revolved around an immobile Earth, and harshly condemned the Italian visionary's treatise, *Dialogue on the Great World Systems*. As punishment for his "blasphemous utterances," Galileo was ordered to repudiate his published observations, and forced to spend the remaining years of his life under house arrest in a villa outside Florence. Galileo died in 1642, but it was not until 1992 that Pope John Paul II acknowledged that the famed astronomer had been wronged by the Catholic Church.

With the passage of time and advancement of science, man gained a better understanding of the interrelationship between Earth and its only natural satellite. The Moon is sometimes called a *terrestrial planet,* because its size and composition are so similar to Earth, Mars, and Venus. The Moon, however, is not an actual planet, merely a satellite, orbiting the Earth once every 27.3 days. Because the Earth simultaneously orbits the Sun, the actual time between new Moons is fixed at 29 days, 12 hours, and 44 minutes. Developers of the modern calendar devised a unit named *moonths,* which eventually became known as months.

The Moon's diameter is only 2,160 miles ($1/4^{th}$ that of Earth's), and its surface area is only $1/13^{th}$ as large. While it is dwarfed by Earth, the Moon is still the second largest satellite in the solar system, and the largest one respective to the size of its mother planet.

The Moon orbits Earth in an elliptical rather than an equatorial plane. At its closest orbital point *(perigee)*, the distance from the Earth to the Moon is 221,463 miles, while at the peak of its orbit *(apogee)*, the distance extends to 252,710 miles.

The Moon follows a *synchronous rotation,* such that the time it takes to rotate around its own axis nearly matches the time necessary for a single orbit around the Earth. As a result of these dual rotations, the same face of the Moon is always visible in the sky—in actuality, due to small variations *(librations)* in its axis of rotation, slightly more than half of the Moon (59 percent) is visible at one time or the other. The remaining 41 percent, referred to as the

Moon's *dark side,* is always out of sight from Earth. This designation is a misnomer; while not visible from Earth, the backside of the Moon receives as much sunlight as the near side. Lunar days last longer than those on Earth, approximately 48 hours in duration.

When the near side of the Moon is pointed toward the Sun, a visible *full Moon* is observed. During the *new Moon* phase, when it is turned away from the Sun, the Moon is invisible to Earth-bound observers.

The rare straight alignment of the Sun, Earth and Moon results in a phenomenon known as an *eclipse.* When Earth is positioned between the Sun and Moon, and casts its enormous shadow over the Moon, a *lunar eclipse* is observable in the night skies. Since the Moon's orbit is inclined approximately five degrees with respect to Earth's orbit, lunar eclipses do not occur with every full moon. A *solar eclipse* is a much rarer occurrence—the result of the Moon passing directly in front of the Sun and casting its shadow on Earth.

While a captive of Earth's gravity, the Moon manages to exert a powerful influence on its mother planet. Lunar gravitational pull on the side of Earth facing the Moon, creates two *bulges* (elevations in sea level), which are constantly rotating. The remaining ocean water pursues those bulges, generating the Earth's high and low sea tides.

The Moon's landscape is barren and its environmental conditions are harsh. The darkened areas visible to the naked eye are lunar plains, known as *maria* (the Latin word for seas). Many experts believe the lunar maria once contained water. For unexplained reasons, most of the maria are found on the near side of the moon, yet occupy only 16 percent of the lunar surface.

The lighter areas observable on a moonlit evening represent highland regions, or *terrae.* The terrae range in height from small hills to mountainous peaks, and dominate the lunar topography

The Moon's surface is pock-marked with craters created by the impact of asteroids and comets. More than 500 million such craters litter the lunar topography—some are only inches in diameter, while the *South Pole Aitken Basin,* located on the far side of the Moon, is 2,250 kilometers-wide and 12 kilometers-deep. The rugged lunar surface is covered with *regolith,* a mixture of fine dust and rocky debris.

Lunar surface temperatures are extreme, averaging 107 degrees Centigrade during the day and -153 degrees Centigrade at night. The Moon's atmosphere is so thin as to be negligible, containing only small concentrations of argon, helium, oxygen, methane, nitrogen, and carbon dioxide, providing scant protection from the Sun's penetrating rays. Because the diffraction of light requires the presence of atmosphere, the lunar sky is invariably a deep black. With its intense sunlight and deep shadows, the lunar climate is inhospitable. With such harsh environmental conditions, it is little wonder that no life forms have been identified on the Moon.

The origin of the Moon is a subject of considerable debate. Strict *Creationists* believe the first Chapter of Genesis clearly explains the divine formation of the Moon. Advocates of the *Fission hypothesis* believe the Moon broke away as a piece from the Earth due to strong centrifugal forces, leaving behind a giant basin that is now occupied by the Pacific Ocean. Others believe the Moon formed elsewhere in the solar system, but was eventually attracted to Earth's gravitational pull—the *Capture hypothesis.* The *Co-formation hypothesis* postulates that the Earth and Moon were formed at the same time from a primordial accretion disk. The prevailing scientific theory is the *Giant Impact hypothesis—Theia,* a planetary body roughly the size of Mars, struck *Protoearth,* and blasted away enough material to form the present day Earth and Moon.

Some astronomers theorize that the Earth once had two Moons, both formed during the *Giant Impact.* The larger of the two Moons, three times wider and 25 times heavier than its counterpart, is believed to have drawn the smaller one into its orbit; the 5,000 mile per hour crash of the smaller planetary body into the larger one resulted in what astronomers refer to as the *big splat.*

The *Co-formation and Giant Impact hypotheses* are both supported by geological analysis of Moon rock. Many of the lunar rocks

8

examined are estimated to be 4.6 billion years old—the same age as Earth's oldest known geological specimens.

Throughout the ages, the Moon has functioned as a chronological and navigational marker. While only half as bright as the Sun, and reflecting just seven percent of its sunlight, a Full Moon is still the brightest object in the night sky; in the *crescent phase*, it is only $1/10^{th}$ as bright as a *full Moon*.

When the Moon is on the horizon, it appears larger, but this is merely an optical illusion, as it is actually 1.5 percent smaller—the result of being further away from the observer by a distance up to one Earth radius. Reaching their maximum height during the winter months, full Moons have provided light for countless generations of nighttime travelers.

Man's fascination with the Moon, stars, and planets evolved into the romantic notion of space flight. In 1865, novelist Jules Verne published *From Earth to Moon*, a fictional story about a lunar mission. In Verne's tale, a rocket ship is launched from a giant cannon called *Columbiad*. With eerie prescience, Verne's manned vehicle took off from Florida, orbited the Moon, and then splashed down in the Pacific Ocean.

A little over a century later, Verne's fantasy would become reality, and his mode of travel distinctly futuristic.

CHAPTER 3

Vergeltungswaffe

To launch a vehicle into space requires momentous thrust to overcome Earth's gravitational force. The age-old, but poorly refined science of rocketry proved to be the only reliable means of generating such thrust.

As early as 1232, the Chinese used rockets fueled by gunpowder during fireworks shows. In 1281, Italians from Bologna used rocket-propelled arrows against their rival-state enemies from Forli, calling the fearsome weapon a *rochetto*, meaning "cylindrical spool of thread."

The earliest rockets were powered by solid fuels, namely gunpowder. While solid fuels could theoretically propel a rocket at sufficient velocity to reach outer space, a major drawback existed—once ignited, there was no control over the vehicle's rate of combustion or amount of thrust.

Born in Russia on September 17, 1857, Konstantin Edvardovich Tsiolkovsky studied mathematics, physics, and astronomy, and then applied much of his creative energy to the study of rocketry. Tsiolkovsky's research led him to believe that a rocket fuel mixture of liquid oxygen and liquid hydrogen would generate considerably more power than black powder. By mixing two volatile liquids in a tight metal chamber and igniting them, Tsiolkovsky theorized that expanding gasses from the explosion could be vented through a hole at high speeds, propelling a rocket and its payload in the opposite direction. The Russian scientist's *Formula of Aviation* defined the relationship between the speed and mass of a rocket as related to its specific propulsion fuel. Tsiolkovsky calculated that a velocity of 18,000 miles per hour was necessary to break the Earth's gravitational force, and also determined that the most efficient way to achieve this goal was to utilize a multi-staged launch rocket.

German mathematics teacher Hermann Julius Oberth, born in Transylvania on June 25, 1894, wrote in detail about space travel in his 1923 treatise, *The Rocket into Interplanetary Space*. Six years later, in a separate publication, *Way to Space Travel*, Oberth outlined the feasibility of using liquid-fueled rockets. That same decade, Oberth and other German rocketeers formed the *Verein fur Raumschiffahrt (VfR)*—the "Society for Space Travel."

Robert Hutchings Goddard, born on October 5, 1882, is widely regarded as America's first true rocket scientist. A native of Massachusetts, Goddard was educated at Worcester Polytechnic Institute, and later taught physics at Clark University.

The New Englander's passion for rocketry began during his childhood and eventually became his life's work. At the age of 27, Goddard published *A Method of Reaching Extreme Altitudes*, which hypothesized that a rocket launched from Earth could reach the Moon. Like many visionaries, the young rocketeer encountered numerous skeptics. In January of 1920, the *New York Times* harshly criticized Goddard's theory that rockets could be utilized for space exploration: "He seems only to lack the knowledge ladled out daily in high schools." Forty-nine years later, as *Apollo 11* raced to the Moon, the famed newspaper published a retraction to its article criticizing Goddard.

Goddard launched his first liquid-fueled rocket from his Aunt's farm in Auburn, Massachusetts in March of 1926. Nicknamed *Nell*, the 10-feet-tall, 10.25-pound rocket was powered by gasoline and liquid oxygen contained in fuel tanks attached by rigid tubes to a small engine. Once the gasoline and oxygen mixture was ignited in the combustion chamber, the hot gasses exploded out a small nozzle at the base of the rocket. Racing into the air at 60 miles per hour, *Nell's* maiden voyage lasted a mere 2.5 seconds, reaching an altitude of only 41 feet, before landing 184 feet down range; nonetheless, it was a milestone in the science of rocketry.

After consulting with a meteorologist at Clark University, Goddard determined that the climate of New Mexico was ideal for year-round rocket launches. In July of 1930, Goddard, his wife, and four assistants, along with a freight car filled with rocket equipment, relocated to a remote area known as Eden Valley, near Roswell, New Mexico. There, Goddard established a rocket science laboratory and test range, which included a launch pad and tower.

Derisively nicknamed "Moony" Goddard by his critics, the ambitious, but intensely private rocketeer received little support from the government. Over the course of four years, philanthropist Daniel Guggenheim provided Goddard with an annual $25,000.00 grant, while famed aviator Charles Lindbergh helped raise additional funds, enabling the rocket scientist to pursue his dreams.

With the passage of time, Goddard's rockets grew more sophisticated, including the installation of gyroscopes. In 1929, Goddard launched the first instrument-containing rocket, which carried a thermometer, barometer, and camera high into the sky. Another of his liquid-fueled rockets broke the speed of sound (Mach 1) in 1935. Goddard subsequently developed a rocket that could travel 1.5 miles into the air at a velocity of 550 miles per hour.

Goddard continued to test rockets at his isolated desert facility for the remainder of his life. In spite of his many successes, Goddard was never able to interest the U.S. military in rocket-propelled weaponry. Eventually granted over 200 patents, Goddard continued to pioneer rocket science technology until his death in 1945. In his final days, he offered a vision of the future: "It is just a matter of imagination how far we can go with rockets. I think it is fair to say, you haven't seen anything yet."

Following in the footsteps of Robert Goddard, Wernher von Braun ultimately became the most successful rocket scientist of the 20th century. Born on March 25, 1912 in Wilintz Germany, von Braun developed a passion for space exploration and rocketry at an early age, devouring the science fiction of Jules Verne and H.G. Wells. After reading those futuristic tales, von Braun was "filled with a romantic urge," and "longed to soar through the heavens and actually explore the mysterious universe." To further his scientific knowledge, von Braun carefully studied the technical writings of Herman Oberth.

In his youth, von Braun caught the attention of villagers by launching rockets into an apple stand and bakery; his father later remembered it as a time of "broken windows" and "destroyed flower gardens." On one occasion, he attached six large, store-bought fireworks rockets to his wooden pull-wagon. After ignition, von Braun attempted to pilot his rocket-propelled vehicle down the sidewalk, as panicked pedestrians leapt out of the way. The police took Wernher in for questioning after his ill-advised experiment, but released him to his father, who promised to take responsibility for the youngster's punishment. In spite of his misadventures, von Braun's curiosity never diminished, and while still a teenager, he joined the rocket club, *Verein fur Raumschiffahrt.*

At age 23, von Braun graduated from Friedrich-Wilhelm University in Berlin, earning a PhD in physics; the subject of his dissertation was liquid-fueled rockets. Early in his career, von Braun worked for the *Society for Space Travel,* along with other rocket researchers, all of whom shared the dream of space travel.

Standing five-feet, eleven-inches-tall, von Braun was handsome and square-jawed, with a thick head of blond hair. Athletic and fluent in several languages, the rocket scientist was charming and gregarious, and cultivated a variety of interests, including music (he played both the piano and cello), philosophy, religion, geography, and politics. Von Braun was also a gifted writer, spell-binding orator, skilled draftsman, and a pilot.

The Treaty of Versailles, which formally ended World War I, punitively limited German arms production. The treaty, however, made no provisions concerning rockets, which were not yet considered viable weapons of war. Accordingly, the German Army assigned artillery officer, Captain Walter Dornberger, the task of assessing how best to exploit this loophole.

In 1932, a year before Adolf Hitler rose to power, von Braun and his fellow researchers were recruited by Dornberger to develop rockets for military use. Von Braun later defended the career decisions of his rocket team as mere stepping stones toward their ultimate dream: "We were interested in only one thing—the exploration of space."

Following World War II, when Nazi atrocities were exposed to the world, von Braun was repeatedly forced to explain his early career path: "...We needed money, and the Army seemed willing to help us. In 1932, the idea of war seemed an absurdity. The Nazis weren't in power. We felt no moral scruples about the possible future use of our brainchild."

As a military employee, von Braun began his tenure at Kummersdorf-West, an artillery proving ground, located south of Berlin. In 1937, von Braun and his rocket development team moved to Peenemunde, on the Baltic coast, near Usedom. There, he was appointed technical director of the Army Research Center, and assigned the task of developing the world's first ballistic missiles.

Shortly after arriving at Peenemunde, von Braun joined the Nazi Party, perhaps naively unaware of the future ramifications of his decision. In later years, he contended that he was "officially demanded" to join the fascist organization, and had he refused, it would have meant abandoning "the work of my life."

"My membership in the party did not involve any political activity," von Braun explained.

In 1940, von Braun joined the notorious paramilitary *Schutzstuffel (SS)*, at the bequest of its infamous leader Heinrich Himmler, and was awarded the rank of Unterstürmfuhrer (Lieutenant). For the remainder of his life, von Braun would downplay his SS membership, pointing out that he did not use his officer's rank on official correspondence, and wore his black dress uniform, with its swastika arm band, only when absolutely necessary. As the war progressed and the Nazi bloodbath expanded, von Braun was promoted to Hauptsturmführer (Captain) and then Sturmbannführer (Major).

The German Army directed von Braun to develop operational ballistic missiles. The end result was the *Aggregat-4 (A-4)*, which the German Propaganda Ministry later renamed the *Vergeltungswaffe-2 (V-2)*, meaning *vengeance weapon*.

The winged V-2 rocket, 46-feet-long and weighing 14 tons, was fueled by ethyl alcohol and liquid oxygen, and stabilized by four fins and four rudders. Two gyroscopes, mounted in the nose beneath the explosive warhead, guided the weapon to its target. The missile was capable of striking targets up to 500 miles away from the launch site. Traveling at 2,500 mph and armed with a 2,200 pound warhead, the V-2 was treacherous and deadly.

After two test failures, in March and August of 1942, the first V-2 was successfully launched on October 3rd of that year. The test missile reached an altitude of 60 miles, and left a lasting impression on rocket scientist, Krafft Ehricke: "It looked like a fiery sword going into the sky…It is very hard to describe what you feel when you stand on the threshold of a whole new era…We knew the space age had begun."

In early July of 1943, von Braun and his military supervisor, Walter Dornberger, briefed Adolf Hitler on the V-2 rocket. The duo informed the Fuhrer that the weapon, armed with 2,000 pounds of explosives, was fully capable of attacking London; furthermore, the British would be powerless to intercept it. With characteristic megalomania, Hitler immediately ordered production of 2,000 V-2 missiles per month.

The first V-2 rockets were launched against London shortly after *D-Day* (June 6, 1944). Famed *CBS News* anchorman Walter Cronkite, who at the time was an *UPI* war correspondent, vividly recalled the frightening attacks, describing the V-2 rockets as "devilish weapons."

A mere five minutes after launch, the devastating rockets terrorized Londoners, who were accustomed to hearing air raid sirens and the drone of approaching German bombers prior to an impending attack. Instead, the unsuspecting civilians were stunned by a "ball of light" and a "terrible crack." One resident described the dilemma posed by the V-2 rockets: "There was no alert…We had no warning at all."

A total of 4,000 V-2 rockets were fired at Allied targets in England, France, and Belgium during the course of World War II; 1,403 of those attacks occurred on London and other targets in southern England. An estimated 5,400 people, more than $2/3^{rd}$ of whom were civilians, died as a result of V-2 attacks.

After Allied bombing raids targeted Peenemunde, the V-2 production facilities were moved to an underground facility in the Harz Mountains, near Nordhausen. Most of the nearly 5,000 workers who participated in the construction of the Nordhausen facility were concentration camp inmates.

The overseer of the Nordhausen construction project, located in a 35 million cubic-feet former anhydrite mine, was a notoriously brutal SS General, Hans Kammler. Prisoners, including Russians, French, Poles, and later Jews, were sent from Buchenwald Concentration Camp to Dora, just outside Nordhausen. The inmates, who were tasked with enlarging the caverns, were subjected to overcrowded, horrendous conditions. The cold, damp, dusty air, absent adequate ventilation, was hazardous to their respiratory systems. There were no running water or sewage facilities, and the raggedly-clad prisoners were forced to sleep in open bunk beds, stacked four high. Consequently, epidemics of pneumonia, dysentery, and typhus were widespread.

Some of the more rebellious inmates attempted to sabotage the rockets during the assembly process; those caught tampering with missiles, as well as those perceived as slackers, were severely beaten and/or executed by their Nazi overseers. An estimated 20,000 prisoners died at Dora/Nordhausen—in the end, more people died during the construction of V-2 rockets than were killed by the heinous weapons during the course of the war.

While von Braun denied playing any role in the decision to use slave labor or in administering the work detail, he was undoubtedly aware of the miserable conditions. Von Braun and his colleagues' association with the atrocities at Nordhausen would be called into question numerous times in later years. Von Braun biographer, Michael Neufield, aptly described the rocket scientist's involvement with the Nazis, as a means to further his dreams of space exploration, a "Faustian bargain."

While serving as a Nazi pawn, von Braun never lost sight of his dream to employ rockets for uses other than weaponry. After he published an article in a scientific journal promoting the use of rockets for international mail delivery, Gestapo Chief Heinrich Himmler ordered the rocketeer jailed for "lack of attention" to the war effort, as well as trumped up charges that von Braun was associating with Communists. Walter Dornberger, von Braun's military supervisor, convinced Hitler to release the rocket scientist from imprisonment, arguing that his expertise was indispensable to the V-2 program.

Von Braun and his colleagues continued to dream of using rocket technology for peaceful means. After an early V-2 test launch, one German scientist was overheard saying: "There goes the world's first space vehicle."

In the spring of 1945, as Germany's defeat appeared all but certain, von Braun gathered his rocket design and development team together to discuss their future. Aware that the end of the war was rapidly approaching, he outlined their options: "We despise the French, we are mortally afraid of the Soviets; we do not believe the British can afford us, so that leaves the Americans."

On May 2nd of that year, von Braun and his colleagues surrendered to American military forces. Ignoring an order, issued six weeks earlier by a desperate Adolf Hitler, instructing the rocketeers to destroy all equipment and paperwork related to the V-2 program, von Braun and his colleagues hid nearly 14 tons of records in an abandoned mine near Bleicherode, and then dynamited the shaft to seal off its contents. After surrendering, the rocket team turned over to U.S. military officials some 3,500 detailed reports and more than 500,000 rocket blueprints stored in the secret hideaway.

The V-2 facility at Nordhausen fell within the Soviet Union's post-war occupation zone. While ultimately recovering only 20 V-2 rockets, the Soviets conscripted their share of German experts in aviation, nuclear energy, electronics, radar, and rocket science. Prior to Soviet occupation of Nordhausen, Major James Pottamill, a ranking officer in the U.S. Army Ordnance Division, orchestrated the removal of parts for nearly 100 V-2 rockets and a "large collection of plans, manuals, and other documents." Those items were transported to the United States, before the Soviets became aware of the subterfuge.

Werner von Braun and his colleagues immigrated to the United States beginning in September of 1945. When a small "advance guard" of higher ranking rocket scientists crossed over the Saar River from Germany to France, en route to a plane that would transport them to the United States, von Braun reminded his colleagues of the consequences of their actions: "Well take a good look at Germany, fellows. You may not see it for a long time to come."

By mid-1946, 118 German rocket scientists, technicians, and their families were settled into their new home at Fort Bliss, Texas, under the direct supervision of the U.S. Army's 9330th Ordnance Technical Service Unit. The massive relocation effort was first named *Operation Overcast*, but later changed to *Operation Paperclip* (in reference to the metal clasps used to bind the Germans' immigration forms). The recruitment and relocation of the German scientists and technicians proved fortuitous, as the U.S. military had no missile technology, even in the planning stages, that was as sophisticated as the V-2 rocket.

Operation Paperclip, authorized by President Truman on September 6, 1946, was administered by the Joint Intelligence Objectives Agency (JIOA) and supervised by the Joint Chiefs of Staff (JCS). The Germans were officially classified as "wards of the Army." Naval Captain Bosquet Wev, Director of the JIOA, had to strong arm American State Department officials, many of whom were troubled over admitting "ex-Nazis" to the United States as "invited guests." Wev argued that the German scientists and technicians conscripted by the Soviet Union were a "far greater security threat" to America than those with "former Nazi affiliations" or current "Nazi sympathies."

The newly-arrived Germans were housed in a remote corner of Fort Bliss, occupying dilapidated barracks serviced by a community mess hall and recreation club. Military personnel were responsible for the security and well-being of the Germans, who had not yet been issued passports. Isolated from the civilian population, none of the immigrants were allowed to leave base unescorted. In large part, the sequestration was a safety precaution, as many civilians in the surrounding area were highly suspicious of their new, "ex-Nazi" neighbors.

Von Braun tried to ease the fears of those Americans who questioned the wisdom of relocating his rocket team to the United States: "We are convinced that a complete mastery of the art of rockets will change conditions in the world in much the same way as did the mastery of aeronautics, and that this change will apply to both civilian and military aspects of the their use."

In 1947, von Braun was allowed to return to Germany to marry his 18-year-old cousin, Maria von Quistor, with the understanding that the couple would immediately return to the United States. During their honeymoon, the couple shared a house with American MPs, who were assigned to keep von Braun from being kidnapped by Soviet intelligence agents.

In 1949, the German scientists and technicians were loaded on a bus and taken across the Mexican border at El Paso. The bus immediately turned around and came back through the border patrol station, where the Germans were issued entrance visas, which could then be used to apply for American citizenship.

The influx of German ingenuity was not limited to the rocket scientists at Fort Bliss. After the conclusion of World War II, the U.S. military relocated nearly 1,600 German scientists, engineers, and technicians to America.

The White Sands Proving Ground (an annex of the Army's Aberdeen Proving Grounds in Maryland), located 40 miles northeast of Fort Bliss, near Los Cruces, New Mexico, served as the launch site for the captured V-2 rockets. In the isolated desert of the Tularosa Basin, von Braun' rocket team merged with *Project*

Hermes, a guided missile program the Army Ordnance Department had previously contracted to *General Electric* in 1944, as an answer to Germany's V-2 program.

On April 16, 1946, the first V-2 rocket was fired at White Sands. From that date through September 19, 1952, 67 V-2s were launched into the New Mexico skies. Instead of explosive payloads, the missiles carried cameras, Geiger counters, and other scientific equipment in their noses. Mice and Rhesus monkeys were also sent aloft to monitor potential health risks of high speed travel at unprecedented altitudes. On July 30, 1946, a V-2 rocket reached the heretofore unimaginable altitude of 100 miles. That same year, another V-2 became the first launch vehicle to detect the ozone layer.

A budget-conscious post-World War II Congress was reluctant to appropriate meaningful funding for rocket research and development, and the German scientists earned a starting pay of only $144.00 per month. Werner von Braun, himself, was paid $9,500.00 per year, with a $6.00 per diem while traveling. Dedicated to their dream of space exploration, the majority of the rocketeers turned down higher paying private-sector jobs and chose to remain as civil service employees.

In 1946, Lieutenant Colonel William E. Winterstern, custodian of the German rocket scientists, posed a far-sighted question to von Braun: "If we could give you all the money you wanted, how long would you need to get man to the Moon and bring him back?" The rocket scientist, who was then a largely unknown figure, asked for some time to contemplate Winterstern's expansive inquiry. Several weeks later, von Braun offered his answer: "Give us three billion dollars and ten years, and well go to the Moon and back."

As the United States established a fledgling missile program, the Soviet Union was busy developing and testing its own rockets. Like Wernher von Braun, Russian-born Sergei Korolev was a visionary, who had established the *Group for Investigation of Reactive Motion* during the 1930s. Korolev, commissioned as a Colonel in the Red Army, traveled to Germany shortly after the end of World War II and supervised the conscription of 150 rocket scientists and technicians. Unlike the United States, which allowed its German immigrants to take an active role in rocket research and development, the Soviets merely learned from their conscripts, before eventually sending them back home. Having salvaged but a handful of V-2s, Soviet scientists utilized German ideas and Russian know-how to develop the next generation of missiles. Korolev would eventually become recognized as the *Chief Designer* of the Soviet missile and space programs.

Having few allies outside its natural boundaries, the Soviet Union did not have available air fields from which to launch nuclear-armed bomber attacks against the United States. To counter the superior American nuclear bomber force, the Soviets decided to develop nuclear missiles as a deterrent.

With the outbreak of the Korean War in June of 1950, American defense spending, which had been significantly curtailed in the years following World War II, dramatically rebounded. As the war raged on the Asian peninsula, the Army missile program was infused with additional funding.

In the mid-1950s, von Braun relocated to the Redstone Arsenal in Huntsville, Alabama, where he was appointed Director of the newly-established Army Ordnance Rocket Center. Accompanied by 115 of his colleagues, their families, civilian *General Electric* employees, and Army personnel with expertise in math, science, and engineering, von Braun set to work developing *Redstone, Jupiter,* and *Pershing* intercontinental ballistic missiles (ICBMS).

The influx of Germans into Huntsville transformed the sleepy North Alabama town into a mecca of scientific research and development. At first, the locals did not quite know what to make of their new neighbors, and jokingly referred to their rapidly expanding community as "Hunnsville." In March of 1955, the German scientists, technicians, and their families were sworn in as U.S. citizens during a mass ceremony in Huntsville.

The Soviet Union, which had already established its first missile launch site, the State Central Test Range, was hard at work developing rocket-propelled weaponry. Led by Sergei Korolev, in 1953, the Soviets unveiled their *R-7* rocket. With 20 individual kerosene and liquid oxygen-burning engines, the powerful R-7 was capable of producing 1.1 million pounds of thrust.

In 1955, President Dwight D. Eisenhower, wary of the escalating *Arms Race*, proposed an *Open Skies* policy to the Soviet Union, whereby the two countries would employ reconnaissance aircraft to monitor each other's military build-up. Soviet Premier Nikita Khrushchev immediately rejected Eisenhower's proposal, believing the U.S. was seeking a convenient means of spying on its rival. By now, Khrushchev was convinced that missile technology would enable the Soviet Union to compete against the United States in the nuclear arms race. In 1956, the Soviet Premier, a master bluffer, boasted that his country was on the verge of possessing "a guided missile with a hydrogen warhead that can fall anywhere in the world." Having established a frightening foothold, the *Cold War* would dominate East/West relations for the next half-century.

Midway through the 1950s, America's German-born rocket scientists had improved V-2 technology, producing the *Redstone* rocket—America's first medium-range ballistic missile, and the vehicle that would ultimately launch the first astronauts into space. Missiles with nuclear warheads, however, remained only a means to an end for Wernher von Braun. A master publicist, von Braun correctly sensed the best way to promote his dream of space exploration was to reach out to the general public. In 1947, he had published *The Mars Project*, a novel which told the story of a mission to the Red Planet, stimulating the curiosity of America's space enthusiasts. From 1952 through 1954, *Collier's* magazine featured an eight-part series on space exploration. Von Braun authored the first article, entitled *Man Will Conquer Space*. In a later edition of the widely-read periodical, von Braun predicted a manned mission to Mars would occur within the next 25 years: "There are no problems involved to which we don't have the answers, or the ability to find them—right now."

By the end of the decade, von Braun's lifelong dream would finally come true. The United States and the Soviet Union would be head-to-head competitors in the multi-billion dollar contest to explore space.

CHAPTER 4
Beep-beep

On October 4, 1957, the world was suddenly and unexpectedly introduced to the *Space Race*. On that brisk fall day, Americans were preoccupied with other activities. The New York Yankees and Milwaukee Brewers were deadlocked, one game apiece, in the World Series, while *CBS* television viewers were looking forward to the season premiere of *Leave it to Beaver.* By the time anyone in the United States was aware that the Soviet Union had launched a satellite, the spacecraft had twice orbited over North America.

Sputnik Zemlyi, "traveling companion of the world," was launched with little fanfare, but the world's first satellite would dramatically change the dynamics between the two superpowers. Orbiting at 25 times the speed of sound, the tiny satellite appeared as a blinking light in the nighttime skies—a visible image of the Soviet Union's head start in space exploration.

Sputnik (its second name was soon dropped) was equipped with a radio transmitter, and its distinctive *beep-beep* sound was audible to short wave radio listeners throughout America. Following an elliptical 141.7 x 588 mile orbit, the Soviet satellite circled Earth once every 96 minutes and 12 seconds. *Sputnik* would remain in orbit, taunting the free world, until January of 1958, when it finally burned up re-entering Earth's atmosphere.

President Dwight D. Eisenhower attempted to diminish the significance of the *Sputnik* launch, describing the satellite as "one small ball in the air, something which does not raise my apprehensions, not one iota." Eisenhower's assessment, however, was in the minority, as reflected in the words of the powerful Senate Majority Leader, Lyndon B. Johnson: "The real meaning of the satellite is that we can no longer consider the Soviet Union to be a nation years behind us in scientific research and industrial capability." The flamboyant Texan, known to Washington insiders as the *Master of the Senate,* issued a shrill warning to his countrymen that the Soviets would soon "be dropping bombs on us from space, like kids dropping rocks from freeway overpasses." Many other influential leaders echoed Johnson's warning. The *Washington Post* likened the *Sputnik* launch to the Japanese bombardment of Pearl Harbor on December 7, 1941; a point in time when the United States had been caught totally unprepared.

Alarmists, clearly in the majority, declared the Russians had mounted an insurmountable lead in the Space Race. Many political and military leaders, all but hysterical, worried the Soviet Union would soon be launching nuclear weapons from space. England's *Manchester Guardian* offered a grave, yet misguided warning: "Russians can now build ballistic missiles capable of hitting any chosen target, anywhere in the world." A proud and bellicose Nikita Khrushchev stoked anxious fires burning outside the Iron Curtain, boasting that the Soviet Union could launch nuclear missiles *anytime* and *anywhere* it wanted.

The profound practical and psychological implications of *Sputnik* jump-started America's entry into the Space Race. Many politicians, fearful of being regarded as *soft* on Communism during the red-baiting, Cold War era, exploited the fears of their fellow citizens. On November 25, 1957, Lyndon Johnson initiated congressional hearings to determine how best to stimulate the country's fledgling space program. In short order, Johnson, who had his eye set on the presidency in 1960, was appointed Chairman of the Special Committee on Space and Astronauts. Other presidential aspirants, including the Democratic junior Senator from Massachusetts, John F. Kennedy, amplified Johnson's clarion call.

Led by scientist and engineer, Sergei Korolev, the Soviet Union was well on its way toward establishing a formidable space program. In 1955, construction had begun on the Baikonur Cosmodrome in the Soviet-controlled Central Asian Republic of Kazakhstan. Protected by heavy military guard, Baikonur was a top secret "closed city," where in totalitarian fashion, research, development, and implementation of the Soviet space program were hidden from the world. Only the cameras of American U-2 spy planes were privy to the activities at Baikonur. With its powerful *R-7* rocket having already proven that it could launch a satellite into orbit, the Soviet Union was preparing to leave its Cold War rival in the starting blocks.

President Eisenhower, ever calm during real or perceived crises, was clearly aware that Soviet rocket technology was vastly overrated, and knew the so-called *missile gap* was politically-inspired fiction. Detailed photographs taken during U-2 flights over the Soviet Union had provided the President with evidence that Khrushchev's dire warnings about the numerical superiority of his country's nuclear missiles were largely boastful rhetoric. Unwilling to publicly reveal the clandestine nature of the U-2 program, Eisenhower played his top secret cards close to the vest, and chose not to refute the errant cries of missile gap proponents.

Just under a month after its inaugural triumph, the Soviet Union launched *Sputnik 2*, a 1,120-pound satellite (the size of a small car), transporting a canine passenger into orbit. *Laika* (Russian for "barker"), the world's first *space dog*, could indeed be heard barking over the satellite radio transmitter—proof positive that living creatures could survive, at least for a short time, in zero gravity. In spite of growing anxiety over the twin Soviet successes, the American press lampooned the satellite as *Muttnik* and *Poochnik*. *Laika* died after four days in orbit, either from oxygen

27

deprivation, overheating, or poison injection, the latter of which the Soviets considered more humane, since the satellite could not be recovered. *Laika's* death enraged American dog owners, who found yet another reason to despise the Godless Communists.

During the next three years, the Soviet Union would launch more *Sputnik* satellites. None, however, would have the same startling impact as the very first one.

America's first attempt to join the Space Race ended in failure. Temporarily shunning the expertise of the German-born rocket scientists at the Army's Redstone Arsenal, the Eisenhower Administration opted to utilize the Navy's *Vanguard* rockets to launch the country's first orbiting satellite. A measure of anti-German prejudice still permeated the government's leadership, so the "made in America" Navy rockets were given the first chance to make history. Werner von Braun shared his disappointment: "This is not a design contest. It is a contest to get a satellite into orbit, and we are way ahead on this."

On December 6, 1957, a large contingent of reporters and cameramen gathered at Cape Canaveral to witness the *Vanguard* rocket attempt to launch a 3.2-pound satellite into orbit. The rocket managed to lift four feet off the ground, before collapsing into a ball of fire. The grapefruit-sized satellite somehow managed to roll away from the launch pad inferno unscathed, prompting *New York Journal American* columnist, Dorothy Kilgallen, to quip: "Why doesn't somebody go out there and kill it?"

The media lampooned the failed launch as *Flopnik, Kaputnik, and Stayputnik.* Von Braun found it increasingly difficult to contain his frustration: "...We could have done this with our Redstone (missile) two years ago...*Vanguard* will never make it...We have the hardware on the shelf...For God's sake, turn us loose and let us do something."

In November of 1957, less than a month before the *Vanguard* fiasco, the government had finally given a green light to the German rocket scientists at Redstone Arsenal, allowing them to participate in the satellite launch program. Eighty-nine days later, on January 31, 1958, *Explorer 1* was launched into space by a *Juno* rocket (a modified *Redstone* missile). The satellite entered an elliptical, 220 x 156 mile orbit, and traveling at 18,000 mph, circled the Earth once every 114.8 minutes. The cylindrical-shaped American satellite, 80 inches long and weighing only 12 pounds, and was mocked by Soviet Premier Khrushchev as an "orbiting grapefruit." The American news media, on the other hand, excitedly exaggerated the significance of the orbital milestone: "The 119 days between *Sputnik 1* and *Explorer* were as important to the U.S....as any similar span in history."

The *Explorer 1* satellite proved to be an unqualified success, orbiting the Earth 58,000 times before burning on re-entry in March of 1970. Among the satellite's accomplishments was the discovery of the *Van Allen Belt*. Utilizing sophisticated sensory equipment, *Explorer 1* verified that a zone of trapped radiation encircled the Earth at altitudes greater than 600 miles—a protective cover against potentially deadly celestial radiation.

The struggling *Vanguard* satellite program suffered another setback on January 25, 1958, when the launch rocket's first stage engine malfunctioned, 14 seconds before ignition. Finally, on March 17th of that same year, a *Vanguard* satellite was successfully sent aloft; the spacecraft, which has measured the Earth and Sun's gravitational fields, solar winds, and atmospheric conditions, remains in orbit, yet today. The last successful *Vanguard* launch occurred in March of 1959, but the beleaguered Navy program's success rate was far from spectacular; only three of its eleven satellites made it into orbit.

On July 29, 1958, President Dwight D. Eisenhower signed into law legislation creating the National Aeronautics and Space Administration (NASA). The National Aeronautics and Space Act of 1958 not only established NASA, but also mandated that "activities in space should be devoted to peaceful purposes for the benefit of all mankind." Keith Glennan, the President of Case Institute of Technology, was appointed as NASA's first Administrator, with a firm mandate from the fiscally conservative Eisenhower to engage in "no reckless spending."

America's fledgling space program was placed entirely under civilian leadership. In addition to Wernher von Braun and his Redstone Arsenal colleagues, NASA also acquired the Army's Jet Propulsion Laboratory, and the Navy *Vanguard* program.

As a further commitment to America's space program, President Eisenhower signed into law the National Defense Act on September 2, 1958. Over the next four years, nearly a billion dollars would be appropriated to fund low interest loans for needy students seeking to become math, science, or foreign language teachers. Federal matching funds were set aside for public and private schools to purchase equipment and materials for teaching those disciplines. Nearly 60 million dollars was earmarked to fund 5,500 graduate fellowships in science, engineering, and foreign languages.

On January 1, 1960, NASA's George C. Marshall Space Flight Center, named in honor of President Eisenhower's World War II mentor, officially went into operation at Huntsville, Alabama's Redstone Arsenal. Wernher von Braun was appointed Director of the NASA facility, supervising 5,500 civil service employees and 1,189 on-site contractors.

NASA also established the Goddard Space Flight Center in Greenbelt, Maryland. The new facility would assume flight control and data retrieval responsibilities for NASA's orbiting satellites.

To fully establish its space exploration program, NASA was in need of a rocket launch facility. In 1946, the Pentagon had identified a 15,000-acre land tract along Florida's Atlantic Coast as the ideal location for a missile launch site. The barrier island, known as Cape Canaveral, separated from the mainland by the Banana River, was isolated and remote, and unlikely to subject the civilian population to the hazards of accidental explosions. Once NASA came into existence, the Long Range Proving Ground at Cape Canaveral not only served as a missile test facility, but also as a space rocket launch site. The earliest manned space flights would lift-off from a section of Cape Canaveral known as *ICBM row*.

The resulting socioeconomic impact on this rather remote section of the southern Atlantic Coast was dramatic. Between 1950 and 1968, the population of Brevard County, Florida increased from 23,000 to 239,000.

Cape Canaveral was ideally located for eastbound space launches over the Atlantic Ocean, allowing rockets to follow the Earth's natural rotation. Relatively near the equator, where the Earth's rotational speed is greatest (1,038 miles per hour), the east coast of Florida provided launched rockets with a leg-up toward achieving the necessary orbital velocity of 17,500 miles per hour.

Even with the birth of NASA, President Eisenhower never regarded manned space flight as a priority of his administration, and was perplexed by the "panic" generated by the *Sputnik* launch. Fiscally conservative, Eisenhower took pride in the fact that during his two-term presidency America had avoided war and maintained a solid defense program, without reckless spending. The President was determined to apply the same austerity to the space program.

While he agreed to authorize the first manned space program, later named *Project Mercury,* Eisenhower refused to support the proposed Moon-landing program *(Apollo).* Wary of the powerful, revenue-consuming *military-industrial complex,* Eisenhower was unwilling to "hock his jewels" to achieve a manned lunar landing. NASA Administrator Keith Glennan privately agreed with the President: "If we fail to place a man on the Moon before 20 years from now, there is nothing lost."

Eager to end the Republican Party's eight-year occupation of the White House, the two front runners for the 1960 Democratic presidential nomination, John F. Kennedy and Lyndon B. Johnson, seized upon the issues of missile development and space exploration to campaign against the so-called *malaise* of the Eisenhower years. Once Kennedy secured the nomination and selected Johnson as his running mate, the Democratic ticket trumpeted the non-existent missile gap as evidence that America's security was jeopardized by Soviet technological advances. President Eisenhower's Science Advisor, James R. Killian, discussed this politically-motivated deception in his memoirs: "The drama of space

31

stirred visions on the part of more than one politician that they might ride rockets to higher political ground."

When John F. Kennedy was elected President in November of 1960, NASA's long-range space exploration program was granted a new lease on life. In February of 1961, a month after his inauguration, the new President appointed James Webb as NASA's new Administrator. A lawyer by training, and a one-time oil company executive, Webb had also served as Budget Director and Under Secretary of State in the Truman Administration. With excellent business and organizational skills, the charismatic and politically adroit Webb successfully lobbied Congress to appropriate generous funding to the space agency. In 1960, a year before Webb's appointment as Administrator, NASA's annual budget was 500 million dollars. By 1965, the figure had grown to 5.2 billion dollars. From 1960 to 1965, the number of employees at the space agency ballooned from 10,000 to 36,000.

The Soviets managed to stay at least one step ahead of the United States during the early years of space exploration. In 1959, alone, the Soviet Union sent three unmanned space probes to the Moon. In January of that year, *Luna 1* became the first spacecraft to pass near the Moon. Missing its intended target by 3,700 miles, *Luna 1* entered into orbit around the Sun, providing the first detailed photographs of the lunar surface. *Luna 2*, launched on September 12th, was deliberately crashed on the lunar surface, marking the first landing by a spacecraft on the Moon. In a marriage of technology and propaganda, at impact, *Luna 2* scattered metal pendants on the lunar surface, effectively marking its territory.

In October of 1959, *Luna 3* entered in a high, elliptical, figure-eight Earth orbit, which propelled the probe around the Moon and back. *Luna 3's* cameras recorded the first images of the Moon's *dark side*, and the Soviets boldly christened two of the observed lunar maria as the *Sea of Moscow* and the *Sea of Dreams*.

In a bold attempt to match the Soviet Union's successes, NASA initiated *Project Mercury* in October of 1958. Abe Silverstein,

Director of the Office of Space Flight Programs, was credited with selecting the name *Mercury*; in Greek mythology, *Mercury*, the Olympic messenger, was the son of Zeus and grandson of Atlas.

The *Mercury* objective was to put a manned spacecraft into orbit and bring the astronaut home safely. Each mission would involve a single astronaut—the pilot would learn to maneuver the spacecraft, while testing the physiological effects of prolonged exposure to zero gravity. At this juncture, some aerospace medicine experts feared prolonged weightlessness could be hazardous, perhaps fateful, to humans.

Strict criteria were established to select America's first astronauts; the candidates had to be less than 40 years of age, under 5' 11" tall (to comfortably fit inside a cramped space capsule), weigh less than 180 pounds, be active duty military pilots (with more than 1,500 hours of jet flight experience), and have earned a bachelor's degree or "the equivalent."

The Eisenhower Administration established the selection criteria to prevent poorly-trained and perhaps undisciplined civilians from applying to become astronauts. In addition to their undeniable bravery, military pilots were accustomed to following orders; a trait that appealed to Eisenhower, the iconic World War II General. Many famed test pilots, who had gained notoriety for setting new jet air speed records in the post-World War II era, were excluded from the astronaut training program. Chuck Yeager, the first pilot to break the sound barrier (Mach 1), was disqualified because he had not attended college. Famed test pilots, Scott Crossfield and Joe Walker, were disqualified because of their civilian status. The veterans seemed hardly disappointed, believing that space flight in a "capsule" was not a genuine test of a pilot's skills, and joked that the astronauts would be little more than "Spam in a can."

Among 540 active military test pilots, only 110 met the astronaut selection criteria. Based upon evaluations by their commanding officers and flight instructors, the list was subsequently narrowed to 69. After being interviewed by NASA officials and informed about the nature of astronaut training, 37 of the pilots elected not to participate. Of the remaining 32, 14 fell out during a series of rigorous physical, mental, and medical tests, leaving a final selection pool of 18 men.

Concerns over the potential health hazards of weightlessness and the impact of powerful transverse G forces during the lift-off and re-entry phases of space flight led NASA medical experts to subject the astronaut candidates to an extensive battery of medical tests, some of which defied explanation. The tests were conducted at the Lovelace Clinic in Albuquerque, New Mexico—a facility specializing in aerospace medicine. John Glenn, who was among the 18 finalists, described the ordeal at the Lovelace Clinic: "They drew blood, took urine and stool samples, scraped our throats, measured the contents of our stomachs, gave us barium enemas, and submerged us in water tanks to record our total body volume. They shined lights into our eyes, ears, noses, and everywhere else. They measured our heart and pulse rates, blood pressure, brain waves, and muscular reactions to electric current. Their examination of the lower bowel was the most uncomfortable procedure I had ever experienced; a sigmoidal probe with a device those of us were tested nicknamed 'steel el.' Wires and tubes dangled from us like tentacles from a jellyfish. Nobody wanted to tell us what some of the stranger tests were for."

The astronaut candidates were also administered a wide battery of psychological tests, including Rorschach ink blots, the Minnesota Multiphasic Personality Inventory, the Thematic Apperception Test, and the Guilford-Zimmerman Spatial Visualization Test. Identifying psychopathology was of paramount importance to NASA officials, who were wary of an astronaut "cracking up" while flying in space.

After eight days at the Lovelace Clinic, the prospective astronauts traveled to the Aeromedical Laboratories at Wright-Patterson Air Force Base in Dayton, Ohio, where their physical fitness was measured on stationary bicycles, treadmills, and by repeatedly stepping up and down off of 20-inch-tall boxes. At the same time, the astronaut candidates were subjected to yet another series of unpleasant physiological tests. Cold water was injected into the test pilots' ears to measure eye movements (nystagmus), and their feet were submerged in buckets of ice water to monitor changes in blood pressure and pulse. To measure lung capacity, the men were required to blow into tubes and keep a column of Mercury lifted for as long as possible. They were also placed inside heat chambers and baked to temperatures as high as 130 degrees Fahrenheit. To measure the pilots' responses to 65,000-feet altitudes, they were required to climb inside special chambers, wearing only partially pressurized suits. Tilt tables were utilized to measure the severity of vertigo experienced by each man, while high speed centrifuges exposed them to gravitational forces of up to G-14 (G-1 equals the normal gravitational pull of the Earth; for every G of acceleration force, an individual is subjected to a multiple of his body weight—a 175-pound man at G-3 experiences a 525-pound force). The pilots were also locked inside a darkened, soundproof isolation chamber for three consecutive hours, without being informed, in advance, of the duration of their sensory deprivation. To assess their capacity for handling crisis situations, each man was tested on the *idiot box*—a contraption featuring multiple, simultaneously activated buzzers and flashing lights; each candidate was timed to see how fast he could extinguish the maddening array of the auditory and visual alarms.

In the end, seven pilots were chosen for *Project Mercury*—Alan B. Shepard, Jr., Virgil I. "Gus" Grissom, Gordon Cooper, John Glenn, Scott Carpenter, Wally Schirra, and Donald "Deke" Slayton. A cross section of the Armed forces was represented—Glenn was a Marine; Shepard, Carpenter, and Schirra were Navy pilots; Grissom, Slayton, and Cooper were Air Force men.

The newly-christened *Mercury 7* made their public debut on April 9, 1959. Sitting behind a raised table at the Dolly Madison House in Washington D.C.'s Lafayette Square, within sight of the White House, the astronauts, clad in civilian coats and ties, responded to questions from eager reporters. *Life* magazine writer, John Dille, characterized the fresh-faced astronauts as "part pilot, part engineer, part scientists, part guinea pig, and part hero." The term "star voyagers" soon became synonymous with the *Mercury 7*.

The astronauts began their new careers at the GS-12 civilian pay grade of $8,300.00 per year, but new found fame brought them a measure of fortune. On behalf of the *Mercury 7*, NASA Public Affairs Officer, Walt Bonney, contacted Leo DeOrsey, a skilled tax lawyer and personal representative for a handful of movie stars. DeOrsey agreed to represent the astronauts pro bono, and eventually negotiated a three-year, $500,000.00 contract with *Life* magazine, whereby the popular periodical was granted exclusive rights to the biographies of the astronauts and their wives. In turn, each astronaut was paid $23,809.52 in three annual installments—nearly tripling their yearly pay. *Life* also agreed to provide life insurance for the men, which otherwise would have been unaffordable, given the high-risk nature of their occupations. As a result of this agreement, *Life* published more than 70 articles about the *Mercury 7* and their families.

In order to fulfill their roles as media darlings, the former test pilots were schooled on social graces, appropriate attire, posture, and speech-making. Michael Collins, who would be selected in a subsequent astronaut class, likened the training to *charm school.*

Wherever the intrepid, clean-cut astronauts traveled, they were greeted as America's best and brightest. Wernher von Braun, who was supervising the design of the rockets that would send the astronauts into space, was impressed by the *Mercury 7:* "They are the most wonderful bunch of people you've ever seen. No daredevils by a long shot, but serious, sober, dedicated, and balanced individuals…"

During the Space Race, image often trumped reality. Separated from their wives and children during exhaustive training sessions at Cape Canaveral, and lured by the temptations of nearby Cocoa Beach, a number of the *Mercury* astronauts behaved in a manner inconsistent with their straight-laced media images. The astronauts' drinking, womanizing, and high speed races in their sports cars were conveniently excluded from the contemporary annals of space exploration. John Glenn, whose squeaky clean persona excluded him from the shenanigans in Florida, confronted his fellow astronauts about the rumors of their misbehavior. Believing the line between duty and play was clearly demarcated, Allen Shepard told Glenn, in no uncertain terms, to butt out of the private lives of his compatriots.

While the United States was initiating *Project Mercury*, the Soviet Union was busy establishing its own manned space program. In March of 1960, cosmonaut training began at the Star Town Facility, located a short distance from Moscow. The cosmonaut candidates were selected from the active roster of military pilots. To maintain ethnic purity, all of the prospective cosmonauts had to be full-blooded Russians. In totalitarian fashion, each cosmonaut was expected to demonstrate absolute loyalty to his country and never question the decisions of his superiors, even during flight.

From an initial pool of 20 pilots, a dozen cosmonauts were chosen, and became known as the *Star Town 12*. The inaugural class included Yuri Gagarin, Victor Gorbatko, German Titov, Georgi Situviv, Andrian Nikolayev, Yeugeni Khrunov, Pavel Popovich, Boris Volyanov, Valeri Bykovksy, Aleksei Leonov, Vladimir Kumarov, and Pavel Balyayev.

The first manned Soviet spacecraft was named *Volstok* (Russian for "upward flowing"). Designed by engineer Oleg G. Ivanovsky, the spherical capsule was attached to a conical-shaped equipment module, which contained telemetry and communication equipment, oxygen and nitrogen tanks, antennae, and retrorockets. When the spacecraft returned home, the equipment module would be jettisoned before the spacecraft re-entered Earth's atmosphere, and the capsule would parachute to a ground landing. For safety reasons, during the earliest space flights, the cosmonauts were ordered to parachute from the capsule before it impacted the ground. With deliberate bravado, Soviet authorities disingenuously reported that each cosmonaut remained with his ship until it landed.

Early on, America's first astronauts were exposed to one of many potential catastrophes associated with space flight. On May 18, 1959, the *Mercury 7* witnessed a test of the *Atlas* rocket that would launch them into space. One minute after liftoff, the giant rocked exploded in the Cape Canaveral skies. John Glenn likened the blast to a "hydrogen bomb going off right over our heads." After a brief period of stunned silence, Alan Shepard eased the tension with his morbid sense of humor: "Well, I'm glad they got that out of the way."

The second unmanned *Mercury* mission, launched on November 21, 1960, also ended in failure, when the *Redstone* rocket lifted only a few inches off the launch pad, and then fell against the supporting tower. As the rocket teetered precariously, the capsule parachutes popped out like a party favor—an embarrassing decoration for what became widely known as the "four-inch flight."

On December 19th of that same year, NASA was finally able to launch an unmanned *MR-1* capsule into space. After reaching an altitude of 131 miles, the spacecraft safely returned to Earth, splashing down in the Atlantic Ocean.

In preparation for manned space flight, NASA experimented with animals. The first passengers were pigs, who were strapped inside *Mercury* capsules and dropped from high altitudes to test the spacecraft's impact resistance. The porkers emerged from the exercise with only mild injuries, which humorously validated the claims of many veteran test pilots—astronauts really were just "Spam in a Can."

On May 29, 1959, NASA launched an Army *Jupiter* missile transporting *Able*, a rhesus monkey, and *Baker*, a South American squirrel monkey, into space. Both monkeys wore electrodes to measure their physiological responses to weightlessness and G-forces during the 300-mile-high flight. After splash down, the rocket's passenger compartment was recovered from the Atlantic Ocean, where both passengers were found tucked away, safe and sound.

The next space explorers were chimpanzees, who were selected because their reaction times were nearly identical to those of human beings. A group of 40 chimps housed at New Mexico's Holloman Aerospace Medical Center were trained for space flight. On January 21, 1961, six of the *astrochimps,* along with 20 handlers and medical specialists, travelled from New Mexico to

Cape Canaveral, in preparation for the first test launches. The now impatient *Mercury* astronauts questioned the need for further test flights; a disgusted Alan Shepard expressed hope that the next launch would result in a "chimp barbecue."

On January 31, 1961, ape number 61, nicknamed *Ham*, an acronym for Holloman Aerospace Medical Center, was launched into space. Strapped in a cockpit seat within a plastic pressure chamber the size of a trunk (designed to simulate conditions inside a spacesuit), Ham endured the 16-minute, 39-second flight, sustaining only a minor injury—a bruised nose that occurred during lift-off or splash down.

Ham's flight was not without misadventure. When the spacecraft's retrorockets were jettisoned too early, increasing re-entry speed to 1,400 miles per hour, the capsule splashed down 130 miles beyond the target zone. At impact, two holes were punched in the capsule, causing it to take on 800 pounds of seawater. It took nearly two hours for Navy helicopters to locate the listing capsule; by then, Ham was in a rage, snarling and biting at his rescuers. During the post-flight press conference, the camera flash bulbs further angered the chimp, who viciously bared his fangs to the world.

While monkeys were actually flying in space, the *Mercury 7* proceeded with training exercises. The astronauts were taken for flights aboard F-100 jets, executing Mach 1.4 dives, and C-130 transport planes, flying parabolas; both exercises exposed them to periods of weightlessness.

Using flight simulators, the astronauts familiarized themselves with the newly designed space capsule. In January of 1959, *McDonnell Aircraft Corporation* had been awarded the contract to build 20 *Mercury* capsules. More than 4,000 suppliers ultimately contributed parts or materials for the spacecraft's construction.

Only six-feet, ten-inches-long and six-feet, two-inches-wide (at its greatest diameter), the 4,300-pound capsule's interior was cramped. Engineers and flight technicians, however, were not particularly concerned about the astronauts' comfort, viewing pilots as superfluous additions to the space flights. The spacecraft's propulsion, altitude, guidance, and re-entry systems were designed to be controlled exclusively by ground-based technicians. The astronauts bristled at the diminished role of the pilot, as Deke Slayton angrily acknowledged: "*Mercury* was designed to operate unmanned." At one point, consideration was given to drugging the astronauts just prior to launch, rendering them immune to space sickness and G-force pain, and also preventing them from pushing buttons and flipping cockpit switches.

"All we need to louse things up is a skilled space pilot with his hands itching for the controls," a Bell Lab engineer groused.

In the end, NASA needed heroes as much as it needed spacecraft, if for nothing more than propaganda purposes. Dissatisfied with their roles as passive capsule occupants, the *Mercury 7* successfully lobbied to modify the spacecraft, including installation of a back-up manual navigation system, a cockpit window, and an escape hatch with explosive bolts. The latter feature was deemed a necessity, as the astronauts did not want to be dependent on others to get them out of the capsule, in the event of an emergency.

Before a manned *Mercury* spacecraft ever took flight, the Soviet Union scored another first. On April 12, 1961, Cosmonaut Yuri A. Gagarin became the first person to orbit the Earth. A former fighter pilot, the 27-year-old Gagarin completed a single orbit, lasting 1- hour and 48-minutes, aboard the *Vostok 1* spacecraft. While in orbit, the Soviet cosmonaut ate, drank, and wrote on a note pad, proving that digestive, metabolic, and neurological functions were not seriously impaired by weightlessness.

After returning to Earth, Gagarin earned effusive praise from Nikita Khrushchev: "You have made yourself immortal." Adding fuel to the propaganda fire, Gagarin boasted: "Let the Capitalist countries catch up to our country."

The Soviet newspaper and Communist mouthpiece *Pravda* boasted that Gagarin's space flight was a "great event in the history of humanity." At the same time, the *Washington Post* echoed the angst of many Americans: "The fact of the Soviet space feat must be faced for what it is, and it is a psychological victory of the first magnitude for the Soviet Union." Over the next 26 months, the Soviets successfully launched five more manned space flights, convincing many that America was hopelessly mired in second place in the Space Race.

After the retrorocket malfunction during the chimp Ham's flight, Wernher von Braun insisted on another unmanned test flight, much to the chagrin of the *Mercury* astronauts. The flight proved successful, with the spacecraft following the correct trajectory and landing 307 miles down range in the Atlantic Ocean. Ever cautious, NASA officials had originally planned to send more chimps into space, but after the Soviets launched Yuri Gagarin into orbit, the United States was pressured into launching its own manned spacecraft.

On May 5, 1961, Alan B. Shepard, Jr. became the first American to travel into space. On the morning of the historic launch, Shepard breakfasted on filet mignon, scrambled eggs, and orange juice, before donning cotton underwear and his spacesuit. The latter, manufactured by *B. F. Goodrich* in Akron, Ohio, was made of plastic and aluminized nylon; a modified version of the Navy *Mark IV* pressurized suit. Inside the space suit, Shepard's core temperature was carefully regulated and his body odor was drawn away through an activated charcoal filter. Life-sustaining oxygen entered the protective garment at the thorax and exited through the helmet. To complete his launch attire, Shepard wore custom-designed gloves, boots, and a helmet—the entire 22-pound outfit cost $5,000.00.

High above the launch pad, aided by back-up pilot John Glenn, Shepard squeezed inside the 4,300-pound space capsule, christened *Freedom 7;* each *Mercury* spacecraft would bear the same number, in honor of America's first seven astronauts. Intermittently obscured by cloud cover, a half-Moon overlooked Cape Canaveral, as Shepard sat atop the *Redstone* rocket, an upgraded version of the famed *V-2,* which was capable of generating 367,000 pounds of thrust. Twin movie cameras were mounted inside the capsule—one to monitor the instrument panel and the other to record Shepard's physiological and emotional responses during the space flight.

Fellow astronaut, Deke Slayton, stationed at the launch control center, was designated as the capsule communicator (Cap Com)—the individual who would maintain a direct radio link with Shepard during his flight. Just prior to lift-off, Slayton was joined at launch control by John Glenn and Gus Grissom. In an adjacent building, Gordon Cooper monitored weather conditions, and was on stand-by to coordinate rescue efforts, in the event of an emergency. Wally Schirra and Scott Carpenter waited at nearby Patrick Air Force Base; they were strapped in the cockpit seats of *F-106* jets, poised to chase the spacecraft after launch.

Another man, whose name would eventually become synonymous with space exploration, was on hand at Cape Canaveral to witness Shepard's historic launch. Television news was still in its technological infancy, and *CBS News* anchorman, Walter Cronkite, was forced to narrate the telecast from the back of a station wagon, which was parked within sight of the launch pad.

The 44-year-old Cronkite was an unabashed space enthusiast. NASA capitalized on media exposure to bolster its space program, and Cronkite became one of the agency's most-valued spokespersons. Designated as a space agency insider, the newsman was privy to specific details about space missions, and established close personal relationships with many of the astronauts.

Cronkite's growing fame during the 1960's paralleled the trajectory of the American space program. By the end of his storied career, Cronkite would be known as "America's anchorman," and the "most trusted man in America." Some media pundits, however, criticized Cronkite's enthusiastic support for space exploration, believing that he was compromising his journalistic objectivity to become a "cheerleader" for NASA.

Cronkite's enthusiasm was readily evident during *CBS* broadcasts, and he made no effort to apologize for his often giddy commentary. Cronkite readily acknowledged complicity in the glorification of the *Mercury 7* astronauts: "We were quite aware that the image that NASA was trying to project was not quite honest.

But, at the same time, there was recognition that the nation need-ed heroes."

Prior to the lift-off of *Freedom 7*, Alan Shepard was confronted with the most basic of human needs. Because the initial *Mercury* flights were of such short duration, the space capsules were not equipped with toilet facilities. When *Freedom 7's* launch was delayed several times, Shepard was forced to urinate inside his space suit; NASA medics shut down the electric sensors, to prevent an electrical short. As he awaited the final countdown, America's first star voyager was stoically philosophical: "I just kept looking around me, remember-ing that everything in the capsule was supplied by the lowest bidder."

The countdown to blast-off was repeatedly delayed by cloud cover and an overheated inverter, which had to be replaced. Strapped in his claustrophobic cockpit *couch*, Shepard's impa-tience escalated: "Why don't you fix this little problem, and light this candle?"

At 9:34 a.m., as 45 million Americans watched on television, the mighty *Redstone* rocket's engines finally roared to life and the ground trembled. At the base of the rocket, solid steel flame deflectors deliberately channeled the exhaust away from the en-gines. Streams of water, delivered at the rate of 35,000 gallons per minute, cooled the deflectors, producing giant steam clouds that partially obscured the launch pad.

As the rocket sped skyward over the Atlantic Ocean, Shepard radioed launch control: "Roger. Lift off, and clock is started."

Eighty-eight seconds after blast-off, the rocket surpassed Mach 1, eventually reaching a maximum velocity of 5,100 miles per hour. Through the capsule's periscope, Shepard was able to identify Florida's west coast, the Gulf of Mexico, mammoth Lake Okeechobee, and the Bahamas.

Shepard's 15-minute flight followed a 302-mile arc, reaching an apogee of 116.5 miles, and ended with splash down in the Atlantic Ocean. He endured five minutes of alternating G-11 forces and weightlessness, before landing 260 miles downrange from Cape Canaveral.

During the course of his history-making flight, Shepard briefly disabled the autopilot and used the manual control stick. Jets of hydrogen peroxide, emitted from nozzles on the side of the spacecraft, allowed him to test all axes of flight—the pitch, yaw, and roll of the capsule. Shepard found the brief interval of weightlessness "pleasant and relaxing," partially dispelling the fears of many NASA medical experts.

During the fiery re-entry into Earth's atmosphere, the external walls of *Freedom 7* soared to 3,000 degrees Fahrenheit. While the interior of the capsule reached 100 degrees (F), the temperature in Shepard's pressurized space suit never exceeded 82 degrees (F). At 10,000 feet, the spacecraft's main parachute opened, and minutes later, Shepard likened the impact of splash down to the force of landing a jet on the deck of an aircraft carrier.

Alan Shepard's inaugural space flight transformed him into an instant hero. The *Mercury 7* astronauts and their wives were invited to the White House, where President Kennedy awarded Shepard the *Distinguished Service Medal* during a ceremony in the Rose Garden. A quarter of a million people lined the streets of New York City during a ticker tape parade honoring the country's first star voyager. The *Freedom 7* capsule was sent for display at the Paris Air Show. For the first time, the United States appeared to be making headway in the Space Race.

On April 10, 1961, some three weeks before Alan Shepard's historic flight, President Kennedy convinced Congress to amend the Space Act, which had been passed during the Eisenhower Administration. Kennedy requested that the Vice-President, rather than the President, serve as Chairman of the Space Council. Having long been passionate about space exploration, Lyndon Johnson readily embraced his new appointment.

On April 20th, eight days after Yuri Gagarin became the first man to orbit Earth, Kennedy charged his Vice-President with answering the following questions: "Do we have a chance of beating the Soviets by putting a laboratory in space, or by a trip to the Moon, or by a rocket to go to the Moon and back with a man? Is there any other program which promised dramatic results in which we could win?" Emphasizing the words *win* and *beat,* Kennedy affirmed that the Space Race was as much political as it was technological.

After convening a special committee, deliberately stacked with advocates of space exploration, the Vice-President formulated his response to the President's inquiries. On April 28th, just eight days after undertaking his assignment, Johnson presented Kennedy with a hyperbole-laden, yet compelling memorandum: "Other nations, regardless of their appreciation of our idealistic values, will tend to align themselves with the country which they believe will be the world leader—the winner in the long run. Dramatic accomplishments in space are being increasingly identified as a major indicator of world leadership...If we do not make the strong effort now, the time will soon be reached when the margin of control over space and over men's minds through space accomplishments will have swung so far on the Russian side that we will not be able to catch up, let alone assume leadership."

On May 25th, only 20 days after Alan Shepard's inaugural space flight, capitalizing on the nation's pride and overwhelming sense of accomplishment, Kennedy took his case directly to the public. Addressing a joint session of Congress concerning "urgent national needs," the President issued a bold proposal: "I believe that this nation should commit itself to achieving the goal, before the end of the decade is out, of landing a man on the Moon, and returning him safely to Earth." Near the end of his speech, Kennedy explained that his proposal would be costly: "Let it be clear that this is a judgment which the members of Congress must finally make. Let it be clear that I am asking Congress to accept a firm commitment to a new course of action—a course that will last for many years and carry very heavy costs—531 million dollars in fiscal '62 and an estimated 7 billion to 9 billion additional over the next 5 years..."

While Kennedy's proposal met opposition from a handful of Republicans, including Senator Barry Goldwater and Representative Gerald Ford, and Conservative Southern Democrats, like Senators Richard Russell and J. William Fulbright, all of whom argued against such mammoth expenditures, the President struck pay dirt with the American public and a clear majority of the lawmakers. Having endured the low point of his presidency a month earlier, during the Bay of Pigs fiasco, Kennedy seized upon an issue that energized fellow Americans and rejuvenated his own political fortunes. The anxiety-provoking impact of a Soviet cosmonaut orbiting the Earth on the American psyche was enormous, as reflected by space historian Gerard J. Degroot's succinct analysis: "Gagarin was Kennedy's *Sputnik*."

Kennedy's declaration was inspiring, but many questioned if it was realistic. With only a single space flight under its belt, NASA had less than nine years to fulfill JFK's dream. Nonetheless, on July 21, 1961, the President signed into law the newly passed Extended Space Program Act, giving birth to *Project Apollo*.

At 7:20 a.m., on July 21, 1961, Virgil I. "Gus" Grissom became the second American to be launched into space. Recalling Alan Shepard's bladder issues during the first *Mercury* mission, Grissom chose to wear a woman's girdle under his space suit, believing that it would better absorb urine, in the event nature called. In a similar vein, Grissom, like his fellow astronauts, consumed a low residue diet for three days prior to their launches, avoiding the urge to defecate during the space flight.

Grissom's 15-minute, 37-second suborbital flight aboard *Liberty Bell 7* reached an apogee of 118.2 miles and a maximum speed of 5,168 miles per hour. Grissom experienced 10 minutes of weightlessness, without suffering any adverse effects. As a result of the astronauts' earlier demands, *Liberty Bell 7* was equipped with an enlarged cockpit window, providing Grissom with a much clearer view during his space flight. After re-entry, the capsule's main parachute opened at 12,000 feet, and seven minutes later, the spacecraft splashed down without incident, ending what appeared to have been a flawless mission.

As the capsule bobbed in the Atlantic Ocean, 302.8 miles down range from Cape Canaveral, Grissom removed his helmet and unbuckled his harness, before completing a post-flight checklist and radioing two nearby Navy *Sikorsky* helicopters to come to his rescue. Suddenly and without warning, the capsule's explosive escape hatch blew.

Activation of the escape hatch, similar in design to the ejection seats of the fighter jets Grissom had flown, required the pilot to a pull out a lock pin, before applying five to six pounds of pressure to the plunger, which detonated 70 explosive bolts and blew the door 25 feet away from the spacecraft. For the remainder of his life, Grissom would insist that he did not purposefully or accidently depress the plunger: "I was minding my own business, when I heard a dull thud."

Seawater poured inside the capsule through the open hatch, forcing Grissom to abandon the rapidly sinking ship. One of the two rescue helicopters managed to snag the capsule, but could not lift the heavy, water-filled spacecraft, and was forced to abandon the rescue operation. *Liberty Bell 7* quickly sank 17,000 feet to the bottom of the Atlantic Ocean, and would not be recovered for 37 years.

While the helicopter crews were preoccupied with saving the capsule, Grissom nearly drowned in the choppy seas, made rougher by the downward draft of the choppers' rotors. Grissom's buoyant spacesuit grew dangerously heavy as seawater poured in through the garment's open neck, as well as the oxygen port that he had mistakenly left unplugged. As he struggled to stay afloat, the astronaut grew dismayed and angered by the rescuers' focus on saving the space capsule. Eventually, one of the helicopter crews lowered a harness and retrieved the exhausted and waterlogged Grissom from the ocean.

Grissom's explanation for the spontaneous detonation of the escape hatch fell on deaf ears among many NASA officials. In subsequent reconstructions of the sinking capsule fiasco, engineers were unable to open the hatch without human intervention, leading many to believe that Grissom had depressed the detonator plunger, either accidently or in a purposeful panic.

On August 6, 1961, Soviet cosmonaut German Titov began a 24-hour space flight, orbiting Earth 17 times. The cosmonaut tested the *Vostok 2* spacecraft's manual altitude control system, and became the first person to photograph Earth from space. Titov also consumed a full meal consisting of bread, liver pate, and peas, while drinking black currant juice. Though not made public by the secretive Russians, Titov suffered severe motion sickness, which partially lessened after he slept through five orbits. Like Yuri Gagarin before him, a heroic Titov was promoted from captain to major.

With two suborbital flights under their belt, NASA was prepared to send a spacecraft into orbit. On September 13, 1961, an *MA-4 Atlas* rocket launched a dummy astronaut into space. The spacecraft orbited the Earth twice, before landing in the Atlantic Ocean target zone, three hours after lift-off.

A second chimpanzee, *Enos*, was launched into space on November 29th of that same year. Enos' flight lasted for three hours, as he orbited the Earth twice and endured 181 minutes of weightlessness. Like his suborbital counterpart, Ham, Enos was trained to perform his cockpit duties based upon operant conditioning. If the chimp pulled the correct levers, he was rewarded with water and banana-flavored pellets. However, if he failed to perform the assigned tasks correctly, painful electric shocks were delivered to the soles of his feet. During the orbital flight, a capsule malfunction caused the chimp to be negatively reinforced with electric shocks, regardless of which lever he pulled. By the time rescue crews reached the capsule in the Pacific Ocean, a terrified and angry Enos had painfully ripped out his still-inflated urinary catheter and torn off his biomedical sensory electrodes. Not surprisingly, the enraged chimpanzee tried to bite his Navy rescuers. Adding insult to injury, during the post-flight press conference, the chimp ripped off his diaper and began fondling himself in front of reporters and television cameras, earning the unfortunate moniker, *Enos the Penis.*

After 10 postponements related to unfavorable weather conditions and equipment malfunctions, John Glenn undertook

America's first orbital space flight on February 20, 1962. The more powerful *Atlas* rocket was used for the first time to launch the *Mercury* capsule into space. Constructed by two California-based companies, *General Dynamics* and *Rocketdyne*, the rocket was capable of generating 360,000 pounds of thrust (compared to the *Redstone's* 76,000 pounds).

The task of placing an astronaut into orbit and bringing him home safely was a riskier proposition than the first two *Mercury* missions. In the event of tragedy, President Kennedy had already prepared a formal statement: "To Mrs. Glenn and members of the Glenn family go my deepest sympathy. It was my pleasure to have known John Glenn. This nation and the entire world share his loss with the Glenn family. Space scientists will revere his pioneering spirit forever."

At 9:47 a.m., after a delay of 2 hours and 17 minutes, *Friendship 7* lifted off the Cape Canaveral launch pad; the momentous event was witnessed by more than 40 million television viewers. NASA had established communication stations around the world, such that Glenn could maintain regular radio contact with Earth. Moving west to east, ground stations were located at Cape Canaveral, Bermuda, the Canary Islands, Nigeria, Zanzibar, a Navy vessel in the Indian Ocean, Australia, Canton Island, Hawaii, the California coast, the White Sands Proving Ground, Mexico, Corpus Christi, and Eglin Air Force Base (in the Florida panhandle). Manning the global tracking stations was a massive undertaking, involving some 19,000 individuals.

Over the course of 4 hours and 56 seconds, travelling at a velocity of 25,730 feet per second, Glenn completed 3 full orbits. At this incredible speed, the astronaut witnessed multiple transitions from day to night, and found that each *space day* lasted only 45 minutes. While in space, Glenn consumed parts of 2 separate meals, proving that digestive and metabolic processes were functional in a weightless environment. During the first orbit, the spacecraft's altitude control system malfunctioned, causing the capsule to drift off course. Shifting to manual control, Glenn was able to correct the errant flight path.

A startling reminder of the dangers associated with space travel arose prior to the conclusion of Glenn's first full orbit. *Friendship 7's* alarm system indicated that the spacecraft's ablative heat shield and compressed landing pack were not engaged in the locked position. If the shield did not remain in place, the capsule would burn up during the re-entry phase. NASA flight controllers did not fully inform Glenn of the seriousness of the situation, an unforgivable sin in the eyes of an experienced pilot. Instead, ground control instructed Glenn not to jettison the retrorockets used to position the spacecraft at the correct angle of re-entry into Earth's atmosphere, with hopes that the metal straps anchoring the rocket pack would help hold the heat shield in place. During the fiery re-entry process, when friction generated by the high temperatures blocked radio transmission from the astronaut to ground control, NASA officials kept their fingers crossed, hoping the heat shield would remain in place. After several anxious minutes, Glenn's voice was heard over the radio, confirming a safe re-entry. While the retrorockets and their supporting straps had burned up, the ablative heat shield remained in place and protected the capsule during re-entry. A furious Glenn, backed by his fellow astronauts, insisted that NASA keep crewmembers fully informed about equipment malfunctions during future missions.

John Glenn returned to Earth an even bigger hero than Alan Shepard. When Glenn visited Washington D.C., 250,000 people lined Pennsylvania Avenue to watch him pass. After being honored at the White House, Glenn addressed a joint session of Congress. The *Friendship 7* space capsule departed on a worldwide tour, publicizing America's space exploration milestone.

The clean-cut, straight-laced, former Marine was the ideal ambassador for the American space program. Charismatic, with excellent communication skills, Glenn proved more valuable as a promoter than a pilot, and President Kennedy soon ordered him removed from the flight roster. Historian, William E. Burrows, perhaps summed it up best: "John Glenn came out of *Friendship 7's* inferno as the Lindbergh of his time."

Over the course of the next 15 months, three additional *Mercury* spacecraft were launched into space, and the duration of the orbital flights progressively increased. Deke Slayton had been next on the flight list, but a cardiac arrhythmia (atrial fibrillation) took him out of the rotation. Slayton, bitterly disappointed by his medical disqualification, was rewarded with the creation of a new position, Coordinator of Astronaut Activities, which kept him closely involved with future space flights.

On May 24, 1962, Scott Carpenter was launched into orbit aboard *Aurora 7.* Carpenter circled the Earth three times and conducted experiments involving liquids in a weightless environment. A malfunction of the automatic flight control system forced Carpenter to pilot the spacecraft. While at the helm, Carpenter burned fuel much faster than anticipated, and at the time of re-entry, failed to fire the retrorockets at the appropriate time, resulting in splash down 250 miles outside the target zone. Anxious NASA officials and television watchers waited for an hour, until Navy rescuers located the space capsule. Carpenter was eventually found floating in a life raft, tethered to *Aurora 7,* the latter of which was on the verge of sinking.

During his post-flight press conference, Carpenter made the mistake of embarrassing NASA by calling attention to the lengthy period of time it took rescuers to locate and recover the capsule: "I didn't know where I was, and they didn't either." NASA officials were already frustrated that Carpenter had wasted fuel and misjudged re-entry, leading Launch Control Coordinator Christopher Craft to grouse: "That son of a bitch will never fly for me again!" Craft's angry declaration proved prescient; Carpenter never again flew in space.

Five months later, *Sigma 7* was launched into orbit. Wally Schirra executed 6 full orbits, twice as many as Scott Carpenter, yet consumed only half as much fuel as his predecessor. Schirra also splashed down right on target, just 4.5 miles from the rescue aircraft carrier—NASA officials described it as a "textbook flight."

On May 15, 1963, *Faith 7,* piloted by Gordon Cooper, was launched into orbit. Cooper established a new record for space travel—22 orbits, over the course of 34 hours and 22 minutes, while traveling 546,167 miles. He also became the first astronaut to fall asleep while in orbit. *Faith 7* was equipped with a television camera, which transmitted the first live orbital shots to viewers below. When the spacecraft's automatic control system malfunctioned, Cooper had to use the control stick to keep the ship steady, while manually firing the retrorockets to enable re-entry. Cooper's cool demeanor and piloting skills allowed him to avert disaster.

As *Project Mercury* wound down, NASA was already planning for the next phase of space exploration. Accordingly, 9 new astronauts were recruited in 1962, followed by 14 more in 1963.

While the general public's attention was riveted on *Project Mercury*, NASA's highly successful unmanned space exploration program moved forward. Launched on August 7, 1959, *Explorer 6* became the first spacecraft to photograph Earth from orbit. *Pioneer 5*, launched on March 11, 1960, entered into orbit around the Sun, between Earth and Venus, and became the first spacecraft to map magnetic fields between the two planets.

Launched April 1, 1960, *Tiros I*, the world's first weather satellite, was equipped with infrared observation technology and television cameras. That same month, the first global navigation satellite, *Transit 1B*, was launched into orbit, allowing American ships at sea to calculate their positions with unprecedented precision. Four and a half months later, the world's first experimental communications satellite, *Echo I*, began circling the Earth. Referred to as a passive communications satellite, *Echo I* functioned as a reflector, but not a transmitter; signals could only be sent to it, and "bounced back" to Earth.

With its successful unmanned space flight program and the introduction of innovative technology, America was becoming more than competitive in the Space Race. By October of 1960, the U.S. had successfully launched 26 satellites into orbit. Moreover, NASA's success rate had dramatically improved; in 1958, all 4 launches failed, 9 of 14 were successful in 1960, and 12 of 17 made it into orbit in 1961.

Space intelligence-gathering took on a new meaning in the early 1960s, when CIA operatives "kidnapped" a Soviet *Luna* probe, while the spacecraft was being displayed at a trade fair in Mexico. The American spies kept the probe overnight, climbing inside the vehicle, thoroughly photographing it, and copying down serial numbers from its key components.

During this same era, American spy satellites were regularly photographing Soviet military installations. Spy film capsules were shot down from the satellites and retrieved in mid-air by Air Force planes using hooking devices to snag the downward drifting photo packages by their parachutes.

As the decade marched forward, America continued to refine its satellite technology. *Telstar I,* designed by *Bell Labs* and *AT&T,* was launched into orbit on July 10, 1962. Powered by solar cells, the satellite transmitted live television broadcasts between the United States and Europe. *Telstar I* gave birth to even more sophisticated communications satellites—*Telstar II, Relay,* and *Syncom.* In July of 1963, *Syncom II* was place in *geostationary orbit,* such that signals could be bounced back and forth from Earth, giving rise to the now familiar phrase: "Live by satellite."

The implementation of geostationary orbits enhanced satellite communications. In a geostationary configuration, a satellite assumes a circular orbit, directly above the Equator, and follows Earth's natural rotation. With an orbital period equal to Earth's rotational period, the satellite appears motionless at a fixed point in the sky (a *stationary footprint*). Today, all communications and weather satellites are placed in geostationary orbits, allowing Earth-based antennae to remain permanently pointed to the same position in the sky.

With advancements in rocket propulsion, guidance, and navigation technology, the dream of exploring *outer* space became a reality. On August 27, 1962, NASA launched *Mariner 2,* which became the first probe to fly directly to another planet (Venus).

NASA did, however, struggle with its early unmanned lunar exploration spacecraft. On April 23, 1962, *Ranger 4* blasted into space, and became the first American spacecraft to reach the Moon's surface; the first and second *Ranger* probes had been stranded in Earth's orbit, when their upper-stage engines failed, and *Ranger 3's* upper-stage engine fired too long, causing the probe to miss the Moon by some 20,000 miles. Unfortunately, *Ranger 4* lost power after crashing on the lunar surface, and was unable to transmit pictures and other much-needed data to Earth.

In September of 1962, President John F. Kennedy delivered a memorable address at Rice Stadium in Houston, Texas. Kennedy reiterated America's goal of landing a man on the Moon before the end of the decade: "Some have asked, why go to the Moon? One may as well ask, why climb the highest mountain? Why sail the widest ocean?"

While many believed JFK's goals were unrealistic, the man responsible for designing the space launch rockets never lost faith. Wernher von Braun, who was firmly ensconced as Director of the George C. Marshall Spaceflight Center at Redstone Arsenal, was certain man would eventually reach the Moon.

Von Braun was actively focused on developing the *Saturn V* rocket—the launch vehicle that would send astronauts to the Moon. Well before people outside of the state of Massachusetts were familiar with John F. Kennedy, von Braun's long range plans were already etched in stone. In early May of 1950, the *Huntsville Times* had informed its readers: DR. VON BRAUN SAYS ROCKET FLIGHTS POSSIBLE TO MOON.

In order for men to land on the Moon, two separate but interrelated spacecraft would have to be developed—a vehicle to travel to the Moon and back, and a second one to land on the lunar surface. Astronauts would have to master rendezvous and docking maneuvers, as well as learn to pilot both spacecraft. With these ambitious goals in mind, *Project Gemini* was formally announced in December of 1961.

Originally called *Mercury Mark II,* the *Gemini* spacecraft, manufactured by *McDonnell Aircraft,* was considerably larger than its predecessor, and consisted of three distinct components—a cockpit capsule for the astronauts; an equipment module containing the electrical power system, propellant tanks, communication/ instrumentation equipment, and drinking water; and the engine compartment.

The symbolism associated with the latest NASA project was readily apparent. In Greek mythology, *Castor* and *Pollux* were the *Gemini* twins, and one of twelve Zodiac constellations controlled by *Mercury.* Like their namesakes, *Gemini* spacecraft would accommodate two-man crews and follow in the footsteps of *Mercury.*

In preparation for the *Gemini* flights and future space exploration, NASA's Manned Spacecraft Center relocated from Langley Field, Virginia to Houston, Texas, giving birth to *Mission Control.* While all space launches would continue to originate from Cape Canaveral, Mission Control would now serve as the permanent center for flight operations.

Texas just so happened to be the home state of one of the space program's biggest supporters—Vice President Lyndon Johnson. As usual, politics followed money, only in grander fashion in the Lone Star State. *Humble Oil* donated a large land parcel to Rice University, while retaining rights to the underground oil and gas reserves. In turn, the university donated 1,000 acres to NASA and sold the space agency an additional 650 acres at $1,000.00 per acre.

With the end of the decade in sight, the space program's astronauts, scientists, engineers, and technicians had their work cut out for them. NASA Flight Director Gene Kranz acknowledged the momentous challenge: "We needed to race to our adolescence, and grow up fast." According to Kranz, the Soviet Union's stunning successes served as a prime motivator: "We were tired of being second."

Project Gemini would serve as an important bridge between *Mercury* and *Apollo.* Before man could travel to the Moon, a number of "firsts" would have to be undertaken, which defined the *Gemini* mission: mastery of steering, maneuvering, docking, and undocking (in preparation for employment of the *Apollo* space capsule and lunar excursion vehicle); measurement of the effects of extended periods of weightlessness on the astronauts' health (lunar missions were estimated to last more than a week, and NASA flight surgeons still worried about the effects of zero gravity—some feared prolonged exposure to weightlessness might be fatal); space walks to test the effectiveness of the astronauts' protective spacesuits (in preparation for walking on the Moon); development and utilization of fuel cells, rather than batteries, to generate electricity and produce water (a necessity for the extended flights to the Moon); testing the maneuverability of the heavier, two-man spacecraft (the *Apollo* missions would be expanded to three-man crews, with an even larger spacecraft); testing the onboard computer navigation and flight systems (the computer systems for *Mercury* had been housed at the flight control center rather than inside the spacecraft); and testing the more powerful *Titan II* rocket that would be used to launch the spacecraft into orbit.

Before the first *Gemini* launch, the Soviet Union's space program continued to make headlines, which caused many Americans to mistakenly believe their country was falling further behind in the Space Race. On June 16, 1963, Cosmonaut, Valentina V. Tereshkova, became the first female to fly in space. Two days earlier, another cosmonaut, Valeri Bykovsky, had been launched into space, awaiting Tereshkova's flight. Once both Soviet spacecraft were in orbit together, the cosmonauts maneuvered to within 11 miles of one another—an important step toward the ultimate goal of rendezvous and docking.

In October of 1964, three Soviet cosmonauts were launched in orbit aboard a *Voskhad 1* spacecraft. To accommodate the first three-man space crew, the Soviets were forced to strip out all but the essential electrical equipment inside a *Vostok* capsule. Even then, inside the confined quarters of the spacecraft, the cosmonauts could not wear their bulky pressurized space suits, and remained in orbit for only 24 hours.

While brief and make-shift, the three-man Soviet mission marked another first in space flight. Even with *Gemini* on the immediate horizon, the United States still appeared to be playing catch-up with the Soviet Union.

The assassination of President Kennedy on November 22, 1963 left NASA officials in a state of mourning; the man who dreamed of landing on the Moon had been suddenly and violently taken away. Wernher von Braun's secretary remembered JFK's assassination as the only time she ever saw her boss shed tears.

Mobilizing its grief, NASA redoubled its efforts to achieve a lunar landing before the end of the decade—a living memorial to the martyred President. On Thanksgiving Day, just six days after as his predecessor's death, Lyndon Johnson announced that the Defense Department's Atlantic Missile Range and NASA's Florida Launch Operations Center would be renamed the *John F. Kennedy Space Center.*

Twenty-two months elapsed between the last *Mercury* flight and the first *Gemini* mission. After two successful unmanned flights, *Gemini II*, christened *Molly Brown*, manned by astronauts Gus Grissom and John Young, was launched on March 23, 1965. Grissom jokingly proposed naming the spacecraft *Titanic*, but NASA officials squelched this idea—the sinking of *Liberty Bell 7* during *Project Mercury* remained too embarrassing of a memory.

The *Gemini* spacecraft performed well, and the astronauts orbited the Earth 3 times, spending 4 hours and 53 minutes in space. While circling Earth, the crew of *Gemini II* chartered new waters, and also managed to court controversy. Utilizing the manual navigation system, they were able to maneuver the spacecraft into higher and lower orbits—a critical requirement for rendezvous and docking with another spacecraft. NASA engineers and flight technicians, however, found it less than amusing when they learned Young had smuggled a corn beef sandwich into the capsule. When Young offered the sandwich to Grissom while in orbit, pieces of meat floated about the cabin and stuck to various instruments, which earned the pair sharp reprimands from NASA leadership.

Just five days before the inaugural *Gemini* mission, the Soviet Union achieved another space exploration milestone, when Alexi Leonov became the first man to walk in space. Tragedy was narrowly averted when Leonov experienced difficulty re-entering the *Voskad 2* spacecraft due to the pressure differential between space and the capsule hatch's air lock mechanism, causing his space suit to inflate (akin to the *Michelin Man*). In a risky move, Leonov released pressure from his suit, and then barely managed to crawl back in the spacecraft, before he was overcome by exhaustion.

Further trouble plagued the Soviet crew, when the spacecraft's automatic guidance system failed during re-entry, causing the capsule to land 2,000 miles beyond the recovery area. While parachute-landing in a snow-covered forest, the spacecraft's radio antenna and beacon were sheared off by tree limbs, making it all the more difficult for rescuers to locate the cosmonauts. Leonov and his crewmate were forced to spend the night inside the frigid capsule, surrounded by hungry timber wolves, until they were rescued the next day.

In early June of 1965, during his *Gemini IV* space flight, Edward H. White became the first American to walk in space. Tethered to the space capsule by life support umbilical lines, White used a nitrogen-powered *zip gun* to move about in zero gravity, while orbiting the Earth at 18,000 miles per hour. When it came time to end the space walk and re-enter the capsule, White expressed disappointment: "It was the saddest day of my life." White and his crewmate, James McDivitt, attempted to rendezvous with a *Titan* second-stage rocket, but were unable to dock with their tumbling orbital companion.

Aboard *Gemini V*, in August of 1965, Gordon Cooper and Pete Conrad spent nearly 8 days in space, orbiting Earth 120 times, setting a new record for the world's longest continuous space flight. While the astronauts conducted further testing of the spacecraft's guidance and navigation system, they were forced to contend with a malfunction of the fuel cells, which had replaced batteries as the capsule's electrical power source.

In December of 1965, *Gemini VI*, with crewmembers Wally Schirra and Tom Stafford, and *Gemini VII*, manned by Frank Borman and James Lovell, orbited Earth at the same time (another first) and maneuvered within a few feet of one another. The two crews were close enough to see each other through their cockpit windows, proving that spacecraft could be properly aligned for docking. The *Gemini VII* crew orbited the Earth 206 times and spent an unprecedented 13 days in space.

In March of 1966, aboard *Gemini VIII*, Neil Armstrong and David Scott completed the first successful orbital docking with another spacecraft; an unmanned Air Force *Agena* upper stage rocket, 180 miles above the Earth's surface. The actual docking procedure went smoothly until the combined spacecraft began to uncontrollably spin and roll. Armstrong alertly jettisoned the *Agena* rocket, but the *Gemini* capsule continued to gyrate, escalating to a rate of one revolution per second.

"We have a serious problem here," Armstrong radioed Mission Control.

Dizzy and disoriented by the spinning spacecraft, the astronauts were on the verge of losing consciousness, when Armstrong elected to fire the re-entry engine system.

"We both knew that if this didn't work, we were dead," Scott recalled.

The last second maneuver worked, and the spacecraft recovered from its death spiral. It was later determined that the near-tragedy was caused by one of the spacecraft's thrusters that was stuck in the *on* position.

Gemini IX was supposed to have been flown by Elliot See and Charles Bassett, but both men were killed in a plane crash en route to the *McDonnell Aircraft* plant in St. Louis on February 28, 1966— the first astronauts to die in the line of duty. Gene Cernan and Tom Stafford ultimately piloted the mission, which launched on June 23rd of that same year. The spacecraft was unable to rendezvous with an *Agena* rocket, after its docking mechanism failed to fully deploy. The space flight was partially salvaged, when Cernan took a lengthy spacewalk.

Michael Collins became the first astronaut to execute a successful docking maneuver with an *Agena* rocket during the *Gemini X* mission. The rendezvous and docking procedures were replicated during the *Gemini XI and XII* flights.

While overshadowed by its *Mercury* predecessors and *Apollo* successors, the 10 manned *Gemini* flights, conducted over a 20-month period, were an essential bridge in American space exploration. Mission Control Flight Director Gene Kranz summed up the legacy of the intermediate program: "*Gemini* developed the tools and technologies we needed to go to the Moon, but even more, *Gemini* was an essential step for the crews and (flight) controllers." Neil Armstrong, who piloted *Gemini VIII*, echoed Kranz's observations: "I believe that *Gemini* was timely and synergistic. It provided millions of hours of real experience in the preparation of space vehicles."

When *Project Gemini* concluded, there were only four full years remaining in the decade. If the United States planned to reach the Moon before 1970, it was sink or swim time for *Project Apollo*.

CHAPTER 5
Luck has no business in space flight

During the *Mercury* and *Gemini* years, the United States and the Soviet Union launched unmanned lunar probes to learn more about the Moon's orbit and topography. Between 1961 and 1965, NASA's *Project Ranger* launched nine such probes—after a series of malfunctions, the final three made it to the Moon, and ultimately transmitted an estimated 17,000 detailed photographs of the lunar surface back to Earth. Utilizing these images, NASA was able to identify prospective manned lunar landing sites.

Project Surveyor followed *Ranger,* with five of its seven probes reaching the Moon, between May of 1966 and July of 1968. On June 2, 1966, the three-legged *Surveyor 1* spacecraft landed on the Moon, transmitting 80,000 photographs, which provided NASA scientists and engineers with crucial data concerning the process of lunar descent. After *Surveyor 2* unexpectedly crashed on the Moon, *Surveyor 3* successfully landed on April 19, 1967, and successfully transmitted 6,300 photographs, as well as temperature and seismological data, back to Earth. The probe's robotic arm also trenched the lunar surface to gauge the composition of the soil.

In 1966, the Soviet Union launched two unmanned probes (*Luna 9* and *Luna 10*). *Luna 9* was the first spacecraft to execute a "soft landing" on the lunar surface, while *Luna 10* became the first spacecraft to orbit the Moon.

Throughout the 1960s, the Cold War remained a virtual stalemate. The threat of mutual nuclear annihilation restricted the United States and Soviet Union to aggressive posturing, while preventing eruption of World War III.

At the height of the Space Race, the two super powers managed to achieve a measure of détente. The 1967 *Treaty on Exploration and Use of Outer Space* waived any country's claim to the Moon, which would be treated like international waters, as the "property of all humankind."

Heading into *Project Apollo,* the Soviet Union was already on the verge of losing the Space Race, a fact largely unbeknownst to the American public. When Soviet Premiere Nikita Khrushchev was deposed in 1965, his successors did not share the space exploration fervor of the *Sputnik* years. In 1966, the sudden death of Sergei Korolev, the Soviet Union's lead rocket engineer and spacecraft designer, during a routine but botched surgical procedure, was a major blow to the country's lunar exploration program.

The *N-1* rocket, the Soviets' designated lunar launch vehicle, proved temperamental. Requiring a volatile mixture of liquid oxygen and kerosene to fuel each stage, the *N-1* was subject to overheating. On four separate occasions, *N-1* test rockets exploded either on the launch pad or shortly after lift-off. In contrast, the American *Apollo Saturn V* performed flawlessly.

Bureaucratic infighting between Soviet scientists and their military supervisors led to frequent project delays. The political philosophy of Communism demanded conformity and did not adequately reward innovation. Failure was often followed by punishment, including imprisonment, physical abuse, and/or execution, while accomplishments were rewarded with propaganda-laden commendations or token medals. In such a dysfunctional system, paranoia was epidemic and corruption was rampant, while the temptation to undermine colleagues to save face (and perhaps one's own life), further undermined progress.

Unlike NASA, which was a non-military agency, the Soviets placed civilian scientists and engineers under military supervision. Many Russian military leaders were far more interested in weaponry than space exploration, and viewed the prospect of a lunar landing as a waste of time and money.

America's manned lunar landing program was named by NASA engineer and project manager, Abe Silverstein: "I thought the image of the god *Apollo* riding his chariot across the Sun gave the best representation of the grand scale of the proposed program." NASA Director James Webb articulated the far-reaching goals of the project: "The *Apollo* requirement was to take off from a point on the surface of the Earth that was traveling at 1,000 miles per hour as the Earth rotated, to go into orbit at 18,000 miles per hour, to travel to a body in space some 240,000 miles distant, which itself traveling 2,000 miles per hour relative to Earth, to go into orbit around the body, and to drop a specialized landing vehicle to its surface. The men were to make observations and measurements, collect specimens...and then repeat much of the outward-bound process to get back home...One such expedition would not do the job. NASA had to develop a reliable system capable of doing this time after time." As straightforward as the objective appeared, the planning and execution of a lunar mission was painstaking and exact, with little margin for error.

The *Apollo* mission to the Moon involved sequential steps— launch, orbiting Earth, docking the space capsule with the lunar exploration vehicle, *trans-lunar injection* (escaping Earth's orbit and traveling to the Moon), lunar orbit, lunar descent, Moon walk, lunar ascent, another docking of the lunar module and space capsule, *trans-Earth injection* (escaping the Moon's orbit and returning to Earth), re-entry in Earth's atmosphere, and splashdown/recovery in the Pacific Ocean. Mechanical failure or pilot error in any of these critical phases could easily result in the death of all three astronauts.

The design and development of the components needed to execute an *Apollo* lunar mission was a team effort, involving hundreds of thousands of designers, engineers, and technicians, both at NASA and in the private-sector. The powerful, three-stage *Saturn V* rocket, which cost 350 million dollars, was responsible for launching the spacecraft into orbit. Conceptualized by Werner von Braun, the *Saturn V* was constructed in a joint effort between *North American Aviation, Boeing, McDonnell Aircraft*, and *IBM*.

Under pressure to reach the Moon by the end of the decade, NASA made the decision to embark upon an "all up approach" with the *Saturn V* rocket. In other words, all three stages of the complex rocket would be tested together "live," on the first flight, rather than individually.

The *Saturn V* was the first American space rocket that was designed and constructed as a civilian-only project, without military supervision. Because of its enormous power, the rocket's monstrous first stage could not be fired at full throttle at the Marshall Center in Huntsville, for fear of shattering windows in nearby residences. Instead, the first stage rocket was transported by barge across the Gulf of Mexico and up the Pearl River to the Mississippi Test Facility (later renamed the Stennis Test Center, in honor of Senator John Stennis). At this isolated, swampy south Mississippi location, the *Saturn V's* most powerful engines were repeatedly test fired.

On January 29, 1964, the first *Saturn* rocket, an abbreviated two-stage missile, blasted off from Cape Canaveral. The rocket successfully launched into orbit the largest payload in history—an empty 37,000-pound rocket stage.

The command service module (CSM), which would transport *Apollo* crews to the Moon and back, was built by *North American Aviation*. The lunar excursion module (LM), brain child of Langley Center aeronautical engineer, John C. Houbolt, was constructed by *Grumman*. *General Electric* designed the fuel cells that powered the spacecraft. *Philco Aerospace Company* equipped Mission Control with flight communication consoles, while *IBM* designed the *Apollo* computer systems.

Economics and politics, the parents and nursemaids of the American space program, eventually came to regard their progeny as a needy step-child. By the latter half of the 1960s, the U.S. Treasury was finding it impossible to fund the Vietnam War, Lyndon Johnson's beloved and all-encompassing *Great Society* social programs, and NASA's enormous budget. The space program soon learned that the government cash cow was not an endless reservoir. By decade's end, expenditures for space exploration would be dramatically reduced.

A small, but vocal segment of the American public condemned the Space Race as a misguided venture. An expanding counterculture of disaffected, mostly young Americans viewed war-making and technology as twin behemoths, which were threatening peace and harmony, while occupying minds and consuming monies that could be better utilized to combat social plaques, like hunger, poverty, and disease. At the same time, African Americans, the most rapidly growing segment of the electorate (a direct result of the Voting Rights Act of 1965), believed that social ills, which disproportionately affected minorities, were being woefully neglected by white men who were more interested in walking on the Moon than helping their fellow man. Civil Rights leader Whitney Young echoed the anti-*Apollo* sentiments of his brethren: "A circus act—a marvelous trick that leaves poverty untouched. It will cost 35 billion dollars to put two men on the Moon. It would take 10 billion dollars to lift every poor person in this country above the poverty standard this year. Something is wrong somewhere."

By early 1967, training for the first *Apollo* mission was well underway. Many assumed the successes of the *Mercury* and *Gemini* programs had paved the way for a smooth transition, while others cautioned against overconfidence. NASA Flight Director, Chris Craft, reminded his colleagues: "We're making it look too easy. I hope we don't end up paying a price, someday, for leaving a false impression."

NASA had miraculously skirted potentially deadly mishaps during the 16 manned spaceflights leading up to *Project Apollo,* and none of the astronauts had been seriously injured. Good fortune had smiled on the American space program, but *Apollo* Flight Director, Gene Kranz, offered a terse warning: "Luck has no business in space flight."

A sense of foreboding haunted *Apollo* during its early days. When the first command service module was delivered to Cape Canaveral, NASA engineers complained about the spacecraft's "shoddy workmanship." Inside the space capsule, bundles of exposed wires were a source of concern to launch pad technicians. Unlike *McDonnell Aircraft*, manufacturers of the *Gemini* spacecraft, *North American Aviation* and *Grumman Aviation*, builders of the command service module and lunar module, refused to share their systems information and schematic drawings with NASA flight controllers, cavalierly bypassing an important step in the safety monitoring process. Astronaut, Jim Lovell, summed up the frustrations of many of his colleagues: "The *Apollo* spacecraft, by even the most charitable estimates, was turning out to be an Edsel." Prior to the first scheduled *Apollo* flight, a total of 20,000 system failures were recorded. A disgusted Gus Grissom, who was slated to command *Apollo 1*, left a lemon inside the flight simulator after completing a training exercise. In spite of these concerns, NASA moved headlong toward the first *Apollo* launch.

On Friday night, January 27, 1967, Grissom and his crewmates, Edward White and Roger Chafee, were strapped in the cockpit of their *Apollo 1* command service module, high above the Cape Canaveral launch pad. The astronauts were busily engaged in a full "dress rehearsal" for the scheduled launch in three weeks. Because of several delays related to malfunctions, the crew had already spent five consecutive hours inside the cramped spacecraft. Grissom, a veteran of *Mercury and Gemini*, was fully aware of the many hazards of space flight: "We flew with the knowledge that if something really went wrong up there, there wasn't the slightest hope of rescue." At the same time, no one was prepared for a catastrophe during a routine training exercise.

At 6:31 p.m., suddenly and without warning, Grissom exclaimed: "Hey!"

Seconds later, Roger Chafee shouted: "Fire in the spacecraft!"

"Fire in the cockpit!" Edward White repeated.

NASA personnel at Cape Canaveral and Mission Control, who were monitoring the training session, could not believe their ears. "We're on fire! Get us out of here!" Chaffee pleaded.

Television monitors showed White vainly reaching for the cockpit hatch. In less than 20 seconds, a flash fire asphyxiated the crew, and their bodies were charred by 2,500-degree (F) flames.

The culprit turned out to be a frayed wire beneath the cockpit seats, which generated a spark in the 100 percent oxygen environment, igniting Velcro, paper flight plans, the polyester foam padding inside the seats, and the astronauts' combustible, nylon space suits. The *Apollo 1* crew had no chance of survival—to illustrate the astronaut's hopeless predicament, in a 16.7-pound per square inch, 100 percent oxygen environment, a lit cigarette will disintegrate in only two seconds. The heat generated by the flash fire was intense enough to melt the steel inside the space capsule.

The spacecraft's ethylene glycol coolant yielded toxic fumes, and Grissom had tried in vain to reach the lever that would have vented the pure oxygen and noxious gases outside the spacecraft. Though equipped with state of the art technology, the space capsule did not have a single fire extinguisher.

Any chance for escape was doomed by the configuration of the exit portal. The spacecraft's outer hatch could not be opened until the inner one had been removed—a painstaking process, requiring the use of a torque wrench. Under ideal, non-emergent conditions, it took the astronauts and support crew 90 seconds to open the hatch. Ironically, Gus Grissom had argued against installing an explosive escape hatch in the *Apollo* spacecraft, perhaps tormented by lingering embarrassment over the sinking of his *Mercury* capsule, six years earlier.

Within seconds of the fire breaking out, the pressurized capsule exploded, fracturing its walls. In vain, a rescue team tried to reach the astronauts, but the intense heat and shock waves from secondary explosions kept them at bay. When launch pad personnel finally gained access to the spacecraft, several of the rescuers burned their hands trying to open the hatch.

Once inside the capsule, NASA technicians witnessed unimaginable horror. Chafee was found strapped in his seat, charred beyond recognition. Grissom and White were found near the hatch,
their melted spacesuits fused together in a gory lump. Grissom
(age 40), White (age 36), and Chaffee (age 31) became the first
direct casualties of the American space program. Grissom and
Chafee were buried at Arlington National Cemetery, while White
was laid to rest at his alma mater, West Point.

After the *Apollo 1* tragedy, all manned spaceflights were halted for 21 months, while NASA tried to figure out what had gone
wrong. An in-house investigatory committee ultimately recom-
mended 1,341 design changes for the *Apollo* spacecraft.

Because it was easier to use a single gas supply to maintain
internal cabin pressure, 100 percent oxygen had been routinely
pumped into all American spacecraft. After the *Apollo 1* tragedy,
the capsule atmosphere was changed to a mixture of 60 percent
oxygen and 40 percent nitrogen to prevent propagation of an
inferno. Flame retardant Velcro, paper, and space suit materials
were also developed, in addition to non-flammable cooling liquids. The capsule hatch was re-designed, providing the crew with
rapid exit capability. In the future, if a fire broke out inside the
spacecraft during training sessions, the astronauts would have at
least a fighting chance at survival.

In the wake of the *Apollo 1* fire, NASA officials were devastat-
ed, and many blamed themselves for the tragedy. *Apollo* Flight
Director, Christopher Craft, was remarkably candid: "We got in
too much of a God-damned hurry. We were willing to put up with
a lot of poor hardware and poor preparation in order to try to get
on with the job, and lot of us knew we were doing that."

Many political leaders, who had grown wary of the enormous
budget strain created by the space program, vented their frustrations on NASA. During congressional hearings related to the
Apollo 1 tragedy, NASA Administrator, James Webb, drew a law-
maker's ire: "The level of incompetence and carelessness we've
seen here is just unimaginable."

North American Aviation, builders of the *Apollo* spacecraft, also shared in the blame. In 1972, the company paid the widows of the *Apollo 1* crew a $650,000.00 settlement.

To honor the memories of Grissom, White, and Chafee, NASA cancelled the *Apollo 1, 2,* and 3 missions. The *Apollo 4, 5,* and 6 missions that followed were all unmanned test flights.

The *Apollo 4* spacecraft was launched on November 9, 1967, marking the first deployment of the powerful *Saturn V* rocket. Witnesses to the lift-off were unprepared for the Earth-trembling roar of the mammoth first stage engines. Sound waves violently shook the *CBS News* television broadcast trailer, located three miles from launch pad 31 A. News anchor, Walter Cronkite, placed his hands against the glass window to keep it from shattering, as ceiling tiles fell down: "My God, our building's shaking here! Our building's shaking! The roar is terrific! This big glass window is shaking...Look at that rocket go...Part of our roof has come in here."

Just 11.5 minutes after blast-off, the *Apollo 4* spacecraft was in orbit. Later in the mission, the third stage *Saturn* rocket was fired, propelling the CSM into a higher orbit. On January 22, 1968, *Apollo 5* was launched into space. During this test flight, an unmanned lunar module accompanied the CSM into orbit. After twin successes, the *Apollo 6* spacecraft endured a series of malfunctions while in orbit, including problems with the guidance system and the third stage rocket. Because of these difficulties, the last unmanned *Apollo* mission lasted only six hours.

Following the *Apollo 1* tragedy, the general public's enthusiasm for lunar exploration showed signs of fraying. A *Harris Poll,* commissioned in July of 1967, revealed that 46 percent of those surveyed opposed a manned lunar mission, with only 43 percent still indicating support. When asked if the *Apollo* project was worth 4 billion dollars per year, only 34 percent answered yes, while 64 percent replied no.

On October 21, 1968, 21 months after the tragic launch pad fire, *Apollo 7* was launched. Astronauts Walter Schirra, Donn Eisle, and

Walter Cunningham spent 10 days in space, orbiting Earth 163 times. The crew conducted the first full test of the CSM, which performed well. The mission, however, was not without controversy. Schirra had been launched into space with a head cold, which he soon transmitted to his crewmates. In zero gravity, the astronauts found their nasal passages would not drain unless they constantly blew their noses—a difficult task while wearing space helmets. The astronauts also complained about the poor quality of their freeze-dried food stores, which escalated into arguments over who was entitled to the tastier meal selections.

Schirra, who had already announced that this would be his last space flight, grew testy with Mission Control, after the crew was instructed to conduct additional, unplanned tests: "I have had it up to here, today. From now on, I am going to be an onboard Flight Director…" Post-mission, Schirra expanded on his frustrations: "I had fun with *Mercury*. I had fun with *Gemini*…I lose a buddy, my next door neighbor, Gus (Grissom), one of our seven; I lose two other guys I thought the world of. I began to realize this was no longer fun. I was assigned a mission where I had to put it back on track like Humpty-Dumpty." Having already made the decision to retire, Schirra's candor had no impact on his career. Eisle and Cunningham were not so lucky, and neither flew in space again.

The Soviet Union endured its own tragic misfortunes during the Space Race. On April 23, 1967, a *Soyuz I* spacecraft was launched into orbit and circled the Earth 18 times. During re-entry, the retrorockets were fired too early, causing the capsule to speed into Earth's atmosphere at a much higher velocity than intended. When the spacecraft's main and emergency parachutes became entangled, the capsule struck the ground at 400 miles per hour, killing cosmonaut Vladimir Komarov.

In March of 1968, Yuri Gagarin, the most recognizable hero of the Soviet space program, was killed while flying a *MIG-15* trainer jet. The famed cosmonaut was honored by having his ashes interred in the Kremlin Wall. On December 8, 1968, an unmanned *Zond 7* spacecraft, scheduled to fly around the Moon, exploded shortly after launch, at an altitude of 27 miles.

Apollo 8, which launched on December 21, 1968, was originally scheduled as a mission to test both the CSM and LM in Earth's orbit. However, construction delays on the lunar module forced a change in plans. Instead, astronauts Frank Borman, James Lovell, and William Anders became the first humans to leave Earth's orbit and travel to the Moon. On December 24, 1968, *Apollo 8* entered a 69-mile-high lunar orbit and provided the first television images of the Moon's surface. The spacecraft spent slightly over 24 hours in orbit, circling the Moon numerous times.

On Christmas Eve, during its ninth orbit, as the spacecraft emerged from the *dark side* of the Moon and television cameras captured Earth in the horizon, astronaut Bill Anders addressed a live television audience: "We are now approaching lunar sunrise, and for all people back on Earth, the crew of *Apollo 8* has a message that we would like to send to you. In the beginning, God created Heaven and Earth. And, the Earth was without form and void; and darkness was upon the face of the deep. And, the spirit of God moved upon the face of the waters. And, God said: 'Let there be light...'"

Over the next few minutes, the *Apollo 8* crew took turns reading the first 10 verses of the *Book of Genesis.* The astronauts had ample reason to call on their faith; prior to launch, NASA experts calculated that the odds of the crew returning home alive were only 50 percent. The astronauts concluded their live broadcast with warm holiday wishes: "Merry Christmas and God bless all of you—all of you on the good Earth."

A stunning photograph of Earth taken during lunar orbit was featured on the cover of *Life* magazine. President Johnson was so enamored with the picture that he sent copies to world leaders, including North Vietnam's Ho Chi Minh.

Lunar mania soon spread. The morning after *Apollo 8's* historic orbit, *Pan Am* initiated its "First Moon Flights Club." For $14,000.00, members could reserve a seat on the airline's proposed commercial *Moon Shuttle,* which *Pan Am's* founder, Juan Trippe, forecast would be operational by the year 2000. Some 93,000 people eventually joined the lunar exploration club, including California Governor and future President of the United States, Ronald Reagan.

Early on Christmas morning, the *Apollo 8* spacecraft blasted out of lunar orbit, a maneuver known as *trans-Earth injection*—the crucial first step in its return home. As the astronauts were leaving the Moon, Jim Lovell radioed Mission Control: "Please be informed, there is a Santa Claus."

On December 27, 1968, *Apollo 8* splashed down in the Pacific Ocean, proving that human beings could travel a quarter of a million miles into space and return home safely. At this point, little doubt remained—the United States was clearly the front runner in the Space Race.

Apollo 9, launched on March 3, 1969, was the first test run for all mechanical components involved in a lunar landing. James A. McDivitt, David R. Scott, and Russell L. Schweickart orbited 119 miles above the Earth in the command service module (CSM), nicknamed *Gumdrop*. While in lunar orbit, Schweickart separated the lunar module (LM), christened *Spider*, from the CSM, and piloted it independent from the mother ship. Schweickart and McDivitt flew in *Spider* for 6 hours, travelling more than 100 miles from the CSM. Schweickart and Scott also took spacewalks, testing the protective suits and life support backpacks that would be utilized during excursions on the lunar surface.

The full dress rehearsal for the first Moon landing began on May 18, 1969, when *Apollo 10* blasted into space, left Earth's orbit, and headed for the Moon. Once in lunar orbit, astronauts Thomas P. Stafford and Eugene Cernan boarded the LM, *Snoopy*, and flew to within 50,000 feet of the Moon's surface. Stafford and Cernan were able to photograph the proposed lunar landing sight, providing NASA engineers and geologists with more detailed information about the regional topography. During the lunar descent, John Young remained alone in the CSM, *Charlie Brown*, and orbited high above his two crewmates.

The *Apollo missions 7, 8, 9,* and *10* had been unqualified successes, setting the stage for the grand prize—a lunar landing.

CHAPTER 6
Amiable strangers

By early 1969, the United States was clearly ahead of the Soviet Union in the quest to land a man on the Moon. The Soviets had been unable to achieve orbital docking capability with their *Soyuz* spacecraft until January of 1969; nearly three years after American astronauts had completed this maneuver during the *Gemini* program. While Wernher von Braun's *Saturn V* had launched four *Apollo* spacecraft into space, the temperamental Soviet *N-1* rocket suffered through multiple test failures; yet another misfire would occur just prior to the July launch of *Apollo 11.*

The Soviets had formulated the logistics for a manned lunar landing, provided they could remedy the problems with their launch rocket. Two cosmonauts would leave Earth's orbit aboard an *L-2 Soyuz* spacecraft—the equivalent of the *Apollo* command service module. Once in lunar orbit, a lone cosmonaut would descend to the Moon's surface in a *L-3* landing craft. In the end, because of repeated complications with the *N-1* rocket, the Soviets would never get an opportunity to actually employ either the *L-2* or the *L-3*.

NASA's third and final unmanned Moon exploration program, prior to the *Apollo* lunar landing, began in August of 1966, and lasted for an entire year. During that time, five *Lunar Orbiters*, all successfully launched into space, transmitted detailed photographs of the Moon's surface, such that NASA experts could search for favorable landing sites. The lunar probes also measured radiation levels and mapped the Moon's gravitational fields. Heading into 1969, John F. Kennedy's vow to land a man on the Moon before the end of the decade no longer seemed impossible.

In December of 1968, Neil Armstrong learned that he would command *Apollo 11*. If the *Apollo 8, 9, and 10* missions were successful, Armstrong would become the first man to walk on the Moon.

Director of Flight Crew Operations, Deke Slayton, was responsible for selecting the *Apollo* spaceflight crews. After informing Armstrong of his selection, Slayton discussed potential crewmates with the newly-appointed *Apollo 11* commander.

On January 4, 1969, Michael Collins and Edwin "Buzz" Aldrin were told they would be joining Armstrong aboard *Apollo 11*. Collins would serve as the command module pilot, while Aldrin would accompany Armstrong to the lunar surface. Five days later, NASA publicly announced the identity of the *Apollo 11* crewmembers.

The *Apollo 11* astronauts were all veterans of *Gemini* space flights. As part of their training, the trio had undergone rigorous studies in astronomy, aerodynamics, rocket propulsion, communications, medicine, meteorology, physics, guidance and navigation, flight mechanics, digital computer science, and geology. The geology training involved worldwide field trips to learn about different types of rocks and various soil compositions. Once they were selected to fly on *Apollo 11*, the three men intensified their training regimen, working 14-hour days, six days per week. On occasion, they worked an additional eight hours on Sundays. Between January 15 and July 15, 1969, the *Apollo 11* astronauts logged a mind-boggling 3,521 training hours.

Michael Collins labored in the *North American Aviation*-built command module simulator, mastering flight correction maneuvers, rendezvous/docking techniques, and preparing for multiple contingency scenarios. Armstrong and Aldrin not only had to familiarize themselves with the command module, but also spent countless hours in the *Grumman*-built lunar module simulator.

Armstrong, Aldrin, and Collins shared certain commonalities; each had been born in the same year (1930), and had fathered three children. They were also skilled pilots and dedicated perfectionists. While working together effectively, the astronauts spent little social or recreational time together. A Cape Canaveral technician remembered their unusual relationship: "Although they were totally competent, they just didn't seem to gel as a team. Usually, when a mission crew was named, they stuck together like glue. But, these three, they never did. When they drove up to the pad for tests, it was always in three separate cars. If we broke for lunch, they always drove away separately. There did not seem to be much camaraderie between the three men. I've always said that they were the first crew who weren't really a crew."

Buzz Aldrin later recalled the distant relationship with his crewmates: "There wasn't anything that particularly drew me to Mike, and Neil and I hardly knew one another." Michael Collins candidly described the trio as "amiable strangers."

Apollo 11 commander, Neil Alden Armstrong, was born on August 5, 1930 in Wapakoneta, Ohio. The eldest of three children, Armstrong was a solid student and an Eagle Scout. He became interested in aviation at an early age, and received his pilot's license at the tender age of 16.

Armstrong temporarily abandoned his studies during his sophomore year at Purdue University to become a fighter pilot in the United States Navy. During the Korean War, Armstrong flew 78 combat missions (120 hours), where he was no stranger to adversity. While making a bombing run in a *F9F Panther*, Armstrong's aircraft was struck by ground fire and also hit a cable the North Koreans had strung across a valley. The cable sheared six feet off of his wing, forcing him to eject from the plane. At the conclusion of his military career in 1952, Armstrong had been awarded the *Air Medal, Gold Star, Korean Service Medal*, and *Engagement Star*.

After the Korean War, Armstrong returned to civilian life and resumed college. In 1955, he graduated from Purdue with an undergraduate degree in aeronautical engineering. Armstrong later earned a Master's of Science in aerospace engineering from the University of Southern California.

After completing his formal education, Armstrong joined the National Advisory Committee on Aeronautics—the forerunner of NASA. As a civilian test pilot, Armstrong flew nearly 900 missions, piloting a wide variety of different aircraft. A fellow test pilot remembered that Armstrong "had a mind that absorbed things like a sponge."

In 1962, Armstrong applied to become an astronaut and was accepted in the second group of nine men who would fly into space. While he was the first civilian to join the astronaut corps, Armstrong found the transition from test pilot to astronaut seamless: "There were some similarities between the two, in the sense that both were always planning and trying to solve problems and devise approaches."

In March of 1966, Armstrong made his maiden spaceflight aboard *Gemini VIII*. During that mission, Armstrong performed the first orbital docking of two spacecraft, and was able to reverse the unexpected, potentially catastrophic loss of control of the capsule and *Agena* docking craft. He was the back-up command pilot for *Gemini XI*, but did not actually return to space until the launch of *Apollo 11*.

During his *Apollo 11* training, Armstrong encountered another potential life or death situation while piloting the lunar landing research vehicle, nicknamed the "flying bedstead." The test vehicle, designed to simulate flight in $1/6^{th}$ G Moon gravity, spiraled out of control at Ellington Air Force Base, when its thrusters malfunctioned. Armstrong ejected just 50 feet from the ground and was safely parachuted a short distance away—his only injury was the result of biting his tongue. The test vehicle had nearly tipped completely over during the crash, which would have ejected Armstrong, head first, into the runway. NASA Flight Director Chris Craft estimated that Armstrong avoided certain death by only $2/5^{th}$ of a second.

Such risks were a way of life for astronauts, and Neil Armstrong's innate stoicism and ability to remain calm during crisis situations served him well. Introverted by nature, Armstrong was confident, but never overbearing. Flight Director, Gene Kranz, who described Armstrong as a "quiet observer" during strategy sessions, nonetheless realized that "when you looked at his eyes, you knew that *he* was the commander, and has all the pieces assembled in his mind."

Command module pilot, Michael Collins, a candid observer of human behavior, had the highest regard for his crewmate: "Neil makes decisions slowly and well. As Borman (another astronaut) gulps decisions, Armstrong savors them—rolling them around on his tongue like a fine wine, and swallowing at the very last moment. Neil is a classy guy, and I can't, offhand, think of a better choice to be the first man on the Moon."

Edwin Eugene "Buzz" Aldrin was born on January 20, 1930 in Montclair, New Jersey. Aldrin's father, a Colonel in the Army Air Corps, was also a record-setting cross-country flyer, who later founded the Air Force Institute of Technology. Ironically, Aldrin's mother's maiden name was Moon. The astronaut's unique nickname was the result of his older sister's inability to pronounce the word brother—instead, she called him *Buzzer.*

Like his crewmate, Neil Armstrong, Aldrin developed a passion for flying at an early age, taking his first plane ride when he was two years old. He also collected rocks—a hobby that served him well during the geology portion of his astronaut training.

After high school, Aldrin received an appointment to West Point, where he graduated third in his class. After college, he joined the Air Force and served as a fighter pilot during the Korean War. Piloting *F-86 Sabers,* Aldrin flew 66 combat missions, and was credited with shooting down two Russian *Mig-15* fighter jets. The June 18, 1953 edition of *Life* magazine featured pictures that Aldrin had taken of an enemy pilot ejecting from the aircraft he (Aldrin) had just shot down.

After the Korean War, Aldrin served as an aerial gunnery instructor at Nellis Air Force Base in Nevada, before the Air Force eventually sent him to the Massachusetts Institute of Technology (MIT), where he earned a Doctorate of Science in aeronautics. Aldrin's particular area of expertise was orbital mechanics, and his 259-page doctoral thesis was entitled *Line of Sight Guidance Techniques for Manned Orbital Rendezvous.*

By the time he earned his graduate degree, Buzz Aldrin was enamored with the space program and longed to join the astronaut corps—influenced by his close friend and fellow West Point alum, Ed White, who had been among the second group of astronauts. Aldrin dedicated a graduate school paper to the *Mercury* astronauts: "Oh, that I were one of them."

Aldrin applied to become an astronaut in 1962, but was not selected during the first go around. A year later, he was accepted among the third group of astronauts, who were slated to train for *Project Gemini.* In November of 1966, Aldrin flew on *Gemini XII,* where he took a 5.5-hour spacewalk—the longest in American history.

Unlike the reticent Neal Armstrong, Aldrin was outspoken and opinionated. He was the most talkative among the *Apollo 11* crew, and readily shared his expertise about orbital docking maneuvers with NASA engineers and fellow astronauts. Consequently, Aldrin was not well liked by some of his peers, who derisively nicknamed him *Doctor Rendezvous.*

Apollo 11 crewmate Michael Collins respected Aldrin's intellect: "Heavy, man, heavy. Would make a champion chess player—always thinks several moves ahead. If you don't know what Buzz is talking about today, you will tomorrow, or the next day." Collins also remembered marathon conversations with his fellow astronaut: "Generally quiet and incapable of small talk, Buzz could get wound up on any of a number of technical pet projects of his, and when he did, he could talk the handle off a piss pot..."

Aldrin courted controversy, when others believed that he was angling to become the first man to walk on the Moon, ahead of mission commander, Neil Armstrong. Aldrin attempted to explain his rational: "Throughout the short history of the space program, beginning with Ed White's space walk, and continuing on all subsequent flights, the commander of the flight remained in the spacecraft, while his partner did the moving around. I had never given it much thought, and had presumed that I would leave the lunar module and step onto the Moon ahead of Neil." Aldrin's misconceptions were given additional weight, when the *Chicago Daily News* and New Orleans' *Times-Picayune* headlined stories in late February of 1969: ALDRIN TO BE THE FIRST MAN ON THE MOON.

In March of that same year, Aldrin became aware that NASA's higher-ups were clearly in favor of Neil Armstrong taking the historic first steps on the lunar surface. A dismayed Aldrin immediately discussed his concerns with the *Apollo 11* commander. As might have been expected, Armstrong was reticent to discuss the situation in detail, but told Aldrin, as *Commander*, he reserved the right to be the first one to step on the Moon. When Aldrin attempted to present his case to Michael Collins, the command module pilot steered clear of the controversy, refusing to offer an opinion. Aldrin later disavowed accusations of self-promotion: "In truth, I really didn't want to be the first person on the Moon."

NASA's leadership team soon clarified matters, announcing that Armstrong would be the first man to walk on the Moon. The politically correct explanations were twofold—Armstrong was a civilian pilot and NASA was a non-military government agency; and, Armstrong's position in the lunar module, nearer the hatch, made it easier for him to exit the spacecraft first. In reality, the personalities of the two astronauts played a significant role in the final decision—Neil Armstrong was better liked, and many NASA officials believed Buzz Aldrin had forcefully lobbied for the honor. The final decision was made by Deke Slayton, Director of Flight Crew Operations, Bob Gilruth, Director of the Manned Space Center, George Low, Apollo Program Manager, and Chris Craft, Director of Flight Operations, during a March 1969 meeting in Houston.

"Look, we just knew damn well that the first guy on the Moon was going to be a Lindbergh...And, who do we want that to be?" Craft asked, before answering his own question, "It should be Neil Armstrong. Neil was Neil—calm, quiet, and absolute confidence. He had no ego."

Aldrin's apparent eagerness ultimately backfired, as reflected in Craft's candid assessment: "On the other hand, Aldrin desperately wanted the honor and wasn't quiet in letting it be known. Neil had said nothing."

On April 14, 1969, the *New York Times* ended all speculation, reporting that Neil Armstrong would be the first man to walk on the Moon.

"Buzz Aldrin was crushed, but seemed to take it stoically," Craft later opined.

Michael Collins, the command module pilot and third member of the *Apollo 11* crew, was born on October 31, 1930 in Rome, Italy. Collins' father, an Army General, was frequently transferred to different duty stations, preventing young Michael from establishing firm roots.

Graduating 185th out of his class of 527 at West Point, Collins never took himself too seriously, as evidenced by his yearbook motto: "Stay casual." After graduation, Collins became an Air Force test pilot, where he learned to fly a variety of aircraft, including long-range nuclear bombers. Like Neil Armstrong and Buzz Aldrin, Collins survived a close call, when he was forced to eject from a burning *F-86* fighter jet.

In 1963, after applying for a second time, Collins was accepted into the astronaut corps. In July of 1966, Collins piloted the *Gemini X* spacecraft, and was the first astronaut to execute an uncomplicated rendezvous and docking maneuver with the unmanned *Agena*.

Unlike many pilots turned astronauts, Collins was introspective and blunt in his self-assessment: "Okay, if you're looking for a handball game, but otherwise nothing special. Lazy, in this group of overachievers, at least—frequently ineffectual, detached, waits for happenings instead of causing them; balances this with generally good judgment and a broader point of view than most."

Collins was the backup command module pilot for the ill-fated *Apollo 1* mission, which ended with the fiery launch pad deaths of the primary crew. Many of the astronauts' families had grown close, and Collins volunteered for the unpleasant task of informing Ed White's wife that her husband had been killed.

Scheduled to be the command module pilot on *Apollo 8*, Collins was grounded after undergoing surgery for a ruptured cervical disk. While recovering from the delicate operation, Collins faced the very real possibility of missing out on subsequent *Apollo* missions, but managed to maintain an upbeat attitude: "I'm not always convinced that everything is going to work out well. On the other hand, there's nothing wrong in acting as if things will work out."

After making a full recovery, Collins was inserted into the flight rotation, culminating in his selection as the command module pilot for *Apollo 11*. He also played an active role in helping design the flight suit patch for the historic mission—a bald eagle with an olive branch in its claws, symbolizing peace, which was depicted approaching the lunar surface, with Earth in the horizon. Unlike past manned spaceflights, only *Apollo 11* was written across the top of the patch—the names of the individual crew members were omitted to symbolize the group effort that went into planning and executing the first lunar landing mission.

On July 5th, 11 days before lift-off, the *Apollo 11* crew greeted the press at Cape Canaveral. Sitting inside a 10 x 12-feet, 3-sided plastic box, with a fan blowing behind them, ostensibly to keep the reporter's germs away, Armstrong, Aldrin, and Collins discussed their forthcoming flight to the Moon. Responding to a reporter's question, Neil Armstrong explained the true meaning of the *Apollo 11* mission: "I think we're going to the Moon because it's in the nature of the human being to face challenges. It's by the nature of his inner soul. We're required to do these things, just as salmon swim upstream."

CHAPTER 7
Good luck and Godspeed

On the morning of July 16, 1969, nearly 1,000 NASA engineers and technicians crowded inside the launch control center at Cape Canaveral, prepared to send *Apollo 11* to the Moon. The *Saturn V* rocket was their "baby," having been pieced together in the eight-acre Vehicle Assembly Building (VAB). Unlike the Soviets, who transported their rockets in stages via rail cars, and then erected them on the launch pad, the entire *Saturn V*, nearly four-stories tall, was driven to the launch pad aboard a giant crawler transporter. The gargantuan vehicle, a diesel-powered adaptation of a strip mining shovel, traveled the 3.5 miles between the VAB and the launch pad over a 110-feet-wide gravel road, at the glacial pace of one mile per hour.

Launch pad 39A featured twin octagonal-shaped concrete pads with steel deflectors, designed to divert the first stage engine flames into trenches lined with a ceramic surface that could withstand temperatures up to 2,000 degrees (F). As a safety precaution, the launch pad was located at Cape Canaveral's isolated Merritt Island, which was surrounded by uninhabited beaches and swampland; experts calculated that a fully-fueled *Saturn V* rocket, exploding on the launch pad, would generate a 3,000-feet-wide fireball and an explosive force equivalent to 500 tons of TNT.

Mission Control in Houston was poised to take responsibility for flight monitoring immediately after lift-off. In a large, window-less room known as the *Trench* (or *Bat Room*), four teams of flight controllers would work around the clock to monitor *Apollo 11* every step of the way to the Moon and back. The room was filled with rows of desks, each containing flight monitors, and the walls were covered with large screens that continuously displayed the location of the spacecraft.

At the center of the activity, Flight Director, Gene Kranz, anxiously awaited the *Apollo 11* launch, wearing one of his wife's distinctive hand sewn vests. The Capsule Commander (Cap Com), a role always filled by a fellow astronaut, was set to establish radio contact with the *Apollo 11* crew immediately after lift-off.

The morning sun reflected sharply off the massive *Saturn V* rocket, generating shimmering heat waves. Those who witnessed *Apollo* launches were invariably awed by the rocket's raw power. Shock waves generated by the *Saturn V* engines literally made the Earth move.

The rocket, 364-feet tall and weighing 5.8 million pounds (as much as a Navy destroyer) consisted of three stages, and housed 91 separate engines and 8,000,000 moving parts. Thirty-five feet in diameter, the gigantic first stage was powered by five *F-1* engines that burned 4.5 million pounds of kerosene and liquid oxygen. The second stage, 30 feet in diameter, housed five smaller rocket engines that consumed one million pounds of liquid hydrogen and oxygen. The third stage (*S IV B*), 22 feet in diameter, contained a single *J-2* engine fueled by 192,495 pounds of liquid oxygen and 39,735 pounds of liquid hydrogen. The three-stage rocket's 11 engines were capable of generating a combined 8.7 million pounds of thrust.

High atop the *Saturn V*, Neil Armstrong, Buzz Aldrin, and Michael Collins were buckled into the cockpit of the command service module, *Columbia*. The lunar module, *Eagle*, was safely tucked away in a compartment just below the CSM. A separate rocket, 33-feet-tall, jutted from the capsule's nose cone—the launch escape systems (LES) would be used to separate the CSM from the *Saturn V*, in the event of a launch pad explosion. A protective shield made of fiberglass and cork separated the CSM from the LES, completely covering the cockpit windows, and leaving the astronauts in semi-darkness, while they awaited the final countdown.

Just to the left of Neil Armstrong's knee was a handle labeled *abort*. Michael Collins could not help but think what would happen if the mechanism was accidently triggered: "Jesus, I can see the headline now—'Moonshot falls in ocean. Mistake by crew, program officials intimate. Last transmission from Armstrong prior to leaving launch pad was oops!'"

With a captive worldwide television audience, including President Richard Nixon, glued to their seats, the melodic voice of NASA Public Affairs Officer Jack King heightened the suspense: "12, 11, 10, 9, Ignition sequence start, 6, 5, 4, 3, 2, 1, 0..."

At 9:32 a.m. the first stage engines of the *Saturn V* lifted *Apollo 11* skyward.

"All engines running...We have liftoff! We have liftoff—32 minutes past the hour—liftoff on *Apollo 11*," King announced.

"Good luck and Godspeed," Cap Com radioed to the crew.

"Thank you very much. We know this will be a good flight," Neil Armstrong replied, as the rocket soared into the crystal clear Florida sky.

Consuming three tons (3,500 gallons) of liquid propellant per second, the first stage rocket generated 7.6 million pounds of thrust, and within a quarter of a second, the astronauts were accelerated from zero gravity to G-4. The launch was the roughest part of the entire mission, as reflected in Michael Collins' radio message, 17 seconds after blast-off: "The beast is felt. Shake, rattle, and roll! We are thrown left and right against our straps in spasmodic little jerks. It is steering like crazy, like a nervous lady driving a wide car down a narrow alley, and I just hope it knows where it's going, because for the first 10 seconds, we were perilously close to the umbilical tower."

The first stage of the *Saturn V* rocket burned for 2 minutes and 40 seconds, launching the spacecraft to an altitude of 200,000 feet. At 9:34:40 a.m., the first stage was discarded and fell 45 miles into the Atlantic Ocean. At the same time, the escape tower and boost protection cover were jettisoned, allowing the astronauts to see outside the cockpit window.

"Yeah, they finally gave me a window to look out," Armstrong announced to Mission Control.

The second stage booster burned for six minutes, lifting *Apollo 11* to an altitude of 606,000 feet, before it was discarded at 9:41:12 a.m. Three minutes later, the third stage rocket fired for the first time, and launched the spacecraft into orbit. Just 11 minutes and 42 seconds after lift-off, *Apollo 11* was in an elliptical, 103.6 by 101.4-nautical mile-orbit, zipping around Earth at 17,400 miles per hour.

"We're showing an orbital weight of the combined vehicles of 297,914 pounds. Based on orbital figures, the orbital period is 1 hour, 28 minutes, 16 seconds," Mission Control notified the astronauts.

Cap Com reported further details: "We have a report on the launch heart rates, now, from the flight surgeon; Commander Neil Armstrong's heart rate 110, command module pilot, Mike Collins' 99, lunar module pilot, Buzz Aldrin's 88. These compare with their first *Gemini* flights—their first lift-off back in the *Gemini* Program—Armstrong's heart rate was 146 at that time, Collins' was 125, and Aldrin's was 110."

The *Apollo 11* spacecraft spent 2.5 hours in a *parking orbit*, as the astronauts went through a series of checklists in preparation for the next leg of the trip. At this point, they were able to remove their helmets and gloves while working and acclimating to zero gravity. Each man moved his head slowly, in an effort to prevent vertigo.

According to NASA medical records, 75.95 % of astronauts vomited upon entering weightlessness, as their vestibular systems adjusted to zero gravity. In a weightless environment, astronauts experienced significant redistribution of blood and other bodily fluids, leading to an increase in heart size, decrease in thirst, electrolyte changes, and increased urine output. The unfortunate ones developed acute urinary retention, necessitating self-catheterization.

Two *IBM* computers, one in the CSM and the other in the lunar module, were primed to assist the crew, as they prepared to head to the Moon. Each computer was state of the art for the time, with 74 kilobytes of memory and a 2.048 MHz clock processer. With 19 keyboard buttons, the 70-pound *Apollo* guidance computer, housed in a 3 x 5 feet box, allowed the crew to measure velocity to $1/1000^{th}$ of a foot per second, enabling them to make precise course corrections. The guidance system was necessary to make exact calculations concerning three moving bodies (Earth, Moon, and spacecraft), all of which influenced the CSM's flight pattern. Instructions for computer programing were printed on plastic-coated, erasure-proof sheets, clipped to metal rings inside the capsule.

After orbiting Earth 1.5 times, the *Apollo 11* crew had completed their assigned duties—it was time head to the Moon.

CHAPTER 8
Like a chicken on a spit

While orbiting Earth, command module pilot, Michael Collins, was responsible for charting *Apollo 11's* path to the Moon. Using a telescope, sextant, and star chart, Collins entered data into the spacecraft's guidance, navigation, and control systems computer. He successfully plotted a flight path by first aligning with *Menkent* (star number 30), and then *Nunki* (star number 37). In order to reach the Moon, navigational readings had to be precise. If *Columbia* exited the Earth's orbit with an incorrect trajectory, the *Apollo 11* crew would be launched into space forever.

At 12:16 p.m., three hours after launch, the third stage of the *Saturn V* rocket fired for a second time. The 5.2-minute engine burn increased the spacecraft's velocity to 24,300 miles per hour, propelling the *Apollo 11* spacecraft out of its Earth orbit—an exacting maneuver, known as *translunar injection.*

"Hey, Houston, *Apollo 11.* That *Saturn* gave us a magnificent ride," Collins radioed Mission Control.

"Roger, *11.* We'll pass that on. And, it certainly looks like you are well on your way now," Cap Com replied.

Thirty-three minutes after translunar injection, the CSM detached from the third stage *Saturn* booster, in preparation for docking with the lunar module. The LM was housed in the lunar adapter, atop the *Saturn V* booster, which Michael Collins likened to "a mechanical tarantula crouched in its hole."

Once the CSM separated from the remainder of the rocket, the four panels on the lunar adapter automatically detached and drifted away into space. Once the CSM was 75 feet distant from the *Saturn* booster, Collins turned the CSM completely around and maneuvered into docking position. Utilizing the CSM reaction control system, Collins carefully approached the lunar module. He inserted the probe located on the nose of the CSM into the drogue atop the LM, which automatically engaged three capture latches. The release of pressurized nitrogen gas caused the probe to retract and pull the lunar module into alignment with the CSM, engaging 12 mechanical latches, which held the two vehicles together in a vise grip.

"That wasn't the smoothest docking I've ever done," Collins reported to Mission Control.

"Well, it felt good from here," a delighted Cap Com replied.

After the docking maneuver was completed, the third stage *Saturn* booster was jettisoned into space, preventing it from the trailing the astronauts to the Moon. The CSM (*Columbia*) and LM (*Eagle*), with a combined weight of 98,000 pounds, were positioned for the three-day trip to the Moon.

Outward bound, *Apollo 11* raced through *cislunar* space at 35,579 feet per second. The gravitational forces of the Earth, Sun, and Moon guided the spacecraft toward its lunar destination. The CSM engines would be fired, as needed, to provide course corrections.

The CSM slowly rotated on its axis at $3/10^{th}$ of one degree per second during the trip to the Moon, making one complete turn every 20 minutes. The continuous rotation was necessary to keep the Sun's rays from melting equipment on one side of the vehicle, while the shaded side froze. In the words of Michael Collins, the spacecraft was "like a chicken on a spit."

The astronauts were able to remove their pressurized suits during the translunar leg of the mission. The bulky suits were stored in bags underneath the cockpit couches, allowing Armstrong, Aldrin, and Collins to move comfortably about in their nylon jumpsuits.

The crew had a number of tasks to occupy their time during the journey to the Moon, including systems monitoring, charging batteries, chlorinating drinking water, and dumping wastewater. There was no bathroom in the cramped spacecraft—urine was collected through a condom catheter and vented outside the capsule, while feces were collected and stored in plastic bags. The astronauts could shave, but there were no showers, and marginal body hygiene was maintained by using disposable wipes.

NASA flight surgeons closely monitored the crew's heart rates, and if necessary, could run electrocardiogram tracings. Aboard the spacecraft, there was a special medical kit containing motion sickness and pain suppression injectors, urinary catheters, first aid ointment, bandages, eye drops, antibiotics, anti-nausea pills, stimulants, oral painkillers, decongestants, anti-diarrheal agents, aspirin, and sleeping pills. A survival kit, which would be utilized in the event of an emergency during lift-off or splash down, contained a life raft, utility knife, drinking water, dye markers, a desalinization kit, and a beacon transceiver.

Columbia's kitchen pantry was stocked with nearly 70 different kinds of freeze dried foods, including beef stew, shrimp cocktail, cream of chicken soup, tuna salad, spaghetti with meat sauce, sausage patties, and pineapple fruitcake. Using a special hot water gun, the astronauts hydrated the plastic food packages before each meal. The menu was varied, but not particularly appetizing— one astronaut described it as "add water, ignore taste." Armstrong, Aldrin, and Collins also had packets of dehydrated coffee, specially prepared to suit their individual tastes.

In the spacecraft's tight quarters, the astronauts were forced to set embarrassment aside. The fuel cells that generated the spacecraft's drinking water failed to permanently bond the hydrogen and oxygen molecules, filling the reservoir with gaseous bubbles. The end result of drinking water was flatulence; an odor Michael Collins likened to "a mixture of wet dog and marsh grass."

At night, the astronauts varied their sleeping arrangements, with one of them strapped in his couch wearing a radio headphone, while the other two slept in hammock-like sleeping bags below the cockpit seats. In zero gravity, the crew had to be restrained while sleeping to prevent floating about and inadvertently activating a cockpit switch or lever.

The crew averaged only five hours of sleep per night. With the sun continually shining, masking external cues that differentiated day from night, their circadian rhythms were disrupted.

The astronauts tolerated weightlessness without any ill-effects, but Collins noted a distinct transformation in his crewmates' appearances: "With no gravity pulling down on loose fatty tissue beneath their eyes, they look squinty and decidedly Oriental. It makes Buzz look like a swollen eyed allergic, and Neil like a very wily, sly one."

Over the course of their eight-day mission, the astronauts absorbed a cut in pay. Neil Armstrong's salary was reduced from $16.00 to $4.00 per day, because he was being "housed and fed at government expense."

At the end of their first day in space, 14 hours after lift-off, the *Apollo 11* crew was already 60,000 miles from Earth.

CHAPTER 9

The most awesome sphere that I've ever seen

On the evening of their second day in space, the *Apollo 11* crew passed the *equigravisphere point*, where the Moon's gravitational pull took complete control of the spacecraft. *Columbia* was now 214,402 miles from Earth and had slowed to a velocity of 2,000 miles per hour. Once under the full influence of lunar gravity, the spacecraft would begin to regain speed.

The highlight of day number two had been the firing of the CSM propulsion engines to make a flight course correction. While four such corrections had been planned, only one was actually required. Michael Collins explained the need to slightly alter the spacecraft's flight trajectory to overcome the forces of nature: "The Sun is pulling us, the Earth is pulling us, the Moon is pulling us—just as Newton predicted they would." As the command module pilot, Collins savored the opportunity to make a course correction: "For three brief seconds of service module engine firing, Mike Collins will be driving, instead of Sir Isaac Newton!"

Mission Control informed the astronauts that an unmanned Soviet spacecraft, *Luna 15,* had been launched on July 13th, and was making a desperate attempt to beat *Apollo 11* to the Moon. NASA reassured the crew that the Russian probe would not interfere with their lunar orbit and landing. Unbeknownst to NASA, the latest Soviet *N-1* rocket had exploded on the launch pad four days earlier, effectively ending the Soviets' manned lunar landing program.

In early evening of the second day, the *Apollo 11* astronauts hosted a 36-minute television broadcast. For the first time, the American public was able to see the astronauts in action, far from home. During the lighthearted broadcast, Buzz Aldrin performed zero gravity pushups and Neil Armstrong stood on his head, while Michael Collins demonstrated how to prepare chicken stew in a weightless environment.

As the astronauts grew closer to the Moon, the changing environment was a source of wonderment. Over 200,000 miles from home, Earth's reflected light, also known as *Earthshine,* was intense enough to illuminate *Columbia's* cockpit.

"It was so bright, you could read a book by it," Collins recalled.

The *Apollo 11* crew shared an unprecedented view of the *Milky Way.* Collins marveled at the celestial panorama: "The sky's full of stars."

At the beginning of day three, the Moon was no longer a distant object in the horizon, and the astronauts searched for the right words to describe what they were seeing. Michael Collins shared his observations with Mission Control: "The Moon I have known all my life—that two dimensional, small yellow disc in the sky, has gone away somewhere, to be replaced by the most awesome sphere that I've ever seen..."

Nearly a quarter of a million miles from home, at least one of the astronauts encountered a sobering reminder of the magnitude of the journey. As he gazed out of *Columbia's* cockpit window, Buzz Aldrin held up his thumb, completely blocking out the image of distant Earth.

On day number four, Cap Com awakened the crew with news from home: "First off, it looks like it's going to be impossible to get away from the fact that you guys are dominating all the news back here on Earth. Even *Pravda,* in Russia, is headlining the mission and calls Neil 'the Czar of the ship…'"

Later that same day, the newly commissioned *Czar* shared his bird's eye observations: "The view of the Moon that we've been having recently is really spectacular. It fills about three-quarters of the hatch window, and of course, we can see the entire circumference, even though part of it is in the complete shadow and part of it is in Earthshine. It's a view worth the price of the trip."

CHAPTER 10

Hello Moon

Near mid-day on July 19, 1969, the *Apollo 11* spacecraft passed behind the Moon. Command module pilot, Michael Collins, fired the retrorockets on the CSM's service propulsion system engines for six minutes, slowing the spacecraft's speed from 5,000 to 3,000 miles per hour, allowing *Columbia* to enter into an elliptical orbit (*LOI-1*) around the Moon.

Attainment of LOI-1 required precision; if the engine burn was not of sufficient duration, the spacecraft could be launched into an uncontrollable elliptical orbit. Conversely, if the engine burned too long, *Columbia* could fall out of orbit and crash on the surface of the Moon.

The CSM engine was fueled by liquid propellants—a hydrazine/dimethylhydrazine mixture and nitrogen tetroxide. Both fuels were hypergolic, detonating on contact with one another, and required no spark.

Within the 60 x 170-mile elliptical orbit, *Columbia* cruised around the Moon at 3,600 miles per hour. Each revolution took about two hours to complete.

"Hello, Moon. How's the old back side?" Collins asked aloud.

Neil Armstrong described the spectacular view: "It looks very much like the pictures, but like the difference between watching a real football game and watching it on television. There's no substitute for being here."

Armstrong and Aldrin called out the names of familiar landmarks on the lunar surface—*Mount Marilyn* (named for astronaut Jim Lovell's wife), *Boot Hill, Duke Island* (named for astronaut Charlie Duke), and *Diamond Back and Sidewinder* (geological formations resembling rattlesnakes).

"Yes, there's a big mother over there, too!" Aldrin exclaimed, pointing out a crater below.

"Come on now, Buzz, don't refer to them as 'big mothers'— give them a scientific name," Collins teased.

"It sure looks like a lot of them have slumped down," Aldrin continued.

"A slumping, big mother? Well, you see those every once in awhile," Collins added.

"Most of them are slumping. The bigger they are, the more they slump. That's a truism, isn't it? That is, the older, they get," Aldrin replied, finally joining in the banter with Collins.

The lunar surface appeared rose-colored to the *Apollo 11* crew, and not nearly as drab as photographs had long suggested. Michael Collins named one crater *Kamp*, using the first initials of his wife and children—Kate, Ann, Michael, and Patricia.

Columbia began its lunar orbit on the backside of the Moon, outside of radio contact range, and NASA officials anxiously awaited the spacecraft's emergence from the *dark side. CBS News* anchorman Walter Cronkite narrated the scene for millions of television viewers: "It is quiet around the world, as the world waits to see if *Apollo 11* is in a successful Moon orbit."

After 23 tense minutes, Armstrong radioed Mission Control: "Houston, *Apollo 11,* over." The fight controllers were ecstatic; lunar orbit was a success.

Five hours into *LOI-1,* Collins fired the retrorockets on the CSM's propulsion system for 17 seconds, slowing the spacecraft, and allowing it to drop into a circular orbit *(LOI-2).* The new orbital trajectory measured 66 x 54 nautical miles, placing the combined CSM/LM spacecraft into a more ideal position for lunar descent.

As the fourth day drew to a close, the *Apollo 11* crew covered their cockpit windows to keep the reflected *Moonshine* from disrupting their sleep. It was time to rest—tomorrow, Neil Armstrong and Buzz Aldrin would walk on the Moon.

CHAPTER 11
Magnificent desolation

A t 8:27 a.m., on July 20, 1969, Buzz Aldrin crawled through the 30-inch-diameter tunnel connecting the CSM to the lunar module, beginning a series of preflight checks. An hour later, Neil Armstrong joined him inside the *Eagle*. When Michael Collins closed the hatch behind them, he was fully aware that he might never see Armstrong and Aldrin again. For the command module pilot, it the marked the beginning of a lonely vigil in lunar orbit.

Armstrong and Aldrin were fully aware of the many potential hazards of a lunar landing, and had been authorized to terminate this risky segment of the mission, if their lives were in immediate danger. Two nights before the launch of *Apollo 11*, Tom Paine, who had succeeded James Webb as NASA Administrator, informed the crew: "If you have to abort, I'll see that you fly the next Moon landing. Just don't get killed."

At Mission Control, 35-year-old flight director Gene Kranz addressed his staff concerning the importance of the day ahead: "Okay, all flight controllers, listen up. Today is our day, and the hopes and dreams of the entire world are with us. This is our time and our place, and we will remember this day and what we do

101

here, always. In the next hour, we will do something that has never been done before. We will land an American on the Moon..."

The flight controllers were all ears, as Kranz continued: "We worked long hours and had some tough times, but we have mastered our work. Now, we are going to make this work pay off. You are a hell of a good team—one that I feel privileged to lead. Whatever happens, I will stand behind every call you will make. Good luck and God bless us today!"

At the White House, President Nixon closely monitored the progress of the *Apollo 11* mission. Nixon, among history's most ardent anti-Communists, was eager to prove American innovations and technologies were superior to the Soviet Union's best efforts. A successful lunar landing would be the ideal way to emphasize the President's point.

Nixon and his closest advisers were thoroughly briefed about the potential pitfalls during this most dangerous leg of the mission. In the event of a catastrophe, the President had a pre-prepared statement: "Fate has ordained that the men who went to explore in peace will stay on the Moon to rest in peace. These brave men, Neil Armstrong and Edwin Aldrin, know that there is no hope for their recovery. But, they also know that there is hope for mankind in their sacrifice..."

At 12:46 p.m., during *Columbia's* 13th lunar orbit, Michael Collins activated a switch, releasing the LM from the docking port. The lunar module, bug-like in appearance, with a cockpit for a thorax and four spindly legs, separated from the mother ship.

"The *Eagle* has wings," Aldrin announced.

The LM, piloted by Armstrong, momentarily hovered near *Columbia,* allowing Collins to inspect its exterior for any signs of damage.

"I think you've got a fine looking machine there, *Eagle,* despite the fact that you're upside down," Collins reported.

"Somebody's upside down," Armstrong quipped.

Now that the *Eagle* appeared structurally sound, Armstrong was given the okay to proceed with lunar descent.

"Okay, *Eagle*. You guys take it easy on the lunar surface," Collins radioed his crewmates. For the next 24 hours, Michael Collins would orbit the Moon, hoping and praying that his crewmates would return safely.

Because of features unique to the Moon, the flight of the lunar module could never be exactly duplicated in the flight simulator. Lunar gravitational pull was not evenly distributed due to heavier subterranean rocks called *mascons*, which exerted magnetic forces strong enough to alter the LM's altitude and direction. In many respects, Armstrong and Aldrin's lunar descent was perilous on-the-job training.

Outwardly calm, Neil Armstrong later recalled his anxiety about the lunar landing: "The most difficult part, from my perspective, and the one that gave me most pause, was the final descent to landing. That was far and away the most complex part of the flight. The systems were heavily loaded at the time. The unknowns were rampant. The systems, in this mode, had only been tested on Earth, and never in the real environment. There were just a thousand things to worry about in the final descent… Walking around on the surface (of the Moon), on a one to ten scale, I deemed a one. The lunar descent, on that scale, was probably a thirteen."

To complicate matters, the *Grumman*-built LM had been plagued by multiple system test failures during the construction process. The first lunar module had not been ready for test flight until March of 1969, less than four months before the *Apollo 11* launch.

The *Eagle*, 23-feet-tall and weighing over 36,000 pounds, was divided into two parts. The lower section housed the descent engine, fuel tanks, storage areas, and the landing gear, while the upper part was home to the ascent engine, fuel tanks, and cockpit. To minimize weight, the lunar module was encased in a thin aluminum shell; the walls were only $5/100^{th}$ of an inch thick. The spacecraft's outer skin was so thin, a pencil could be poked through it, leading astronaut Jim McDivitt to describe the LM as a "tissue paper spacecraft." The lunar module's sparsely decorated interior was sprayed with a dull blue-gray fire-resistant coating. To further reduce weight, the interior plumbing and wire bundles were fully exposed.

"The LM flight deck was about as charming as the cab of a diesel locomotive," Aldrin joked.

To conserve space and lessen weight, the *Eagle* had no seats, forcing Armstrong and Aldrin to stand during flight, held in place by elastic cords. During the early stages of the lunar descent, the LM was flown in a sideways position, with its two triangular-shaped cockpit windows facing the Moon's cratered surface. When the spacecraft reached the designated area, Armstrong would reposition the LM into the legs-down mode.

After making a full lunar orbit, Armstrong and Aldrin received instructions from Mission Control: "*Eagle,* Houston. You are a go for *DOI (descent orbit insertion).*"

Armstrong then initiated a 30-second DOI engine burn, lowering the LM's orbit to eight miles above the Moon's craggy surface.

"*Eagle,* Houston. If you read, you're go for a powered descent," Cap Com, Charlie Duke, radioed.

The combination of static and a three-second radio delay made it difficult for Armstrong and Aldrin to hear the instructions from Mission Control. Collins, orbiting 50 miles above his crewmates, alertly relayed the message: "*Eagle,* this is *Columbia.* They just gave you a go for powered descent."

Armstrong responded by firing the power descent engine, positioning the lunar module for landing. At the same time, Aldrin activated a 16-millimeter movie camera, located in his cockpit window, to record the historic approach.

Mare Tranquilitatis (the *Sea of Tranquility*) was the *Eagle's* predetermined landing spot. One degree above the Moon's equator and 23 degrees east of an arbitrary line running from the North to the South Pole, the *Sea of Tranquility* was thought to be free of large boulders and level enough for a smooth landing.

Approaching the landing zone, 33,500 feet above the lunar surface, the *Eagle's* computer systems overloaded, sounding a *1202 alarm.* While the LM's computer was state of the art for the year

1969, with a 64K memory and 36,864 fixed-word memory, the sheer volume of incoming data suddenly overwhelmed its capabilities. The computer experts at Mission Control, led by 26-year-old Steve Bales, the ranking expert on the LM's guidance systems, concluded that the alarm was not indicative of any serious problem. Flight Control soon advised Armstrong and Aldrin to disregard the warning, classifying it as an *acceptable risk.*

The *Eagle* continued its descent at a rate of 30 feet per second. When the LM was 1,000 feet above its designated landing point, Armstrong realized the area was uneven and filled with lunar rocks. With his fuel supply dwindling, the *Apollo 11* commander had little time to find a smoother landing place.

"We could have tried to land there, and we might have gotten away with it. It was a fairly steep slope, and it was covered with very big rocks, and it just wasn't a very good place to go. You know, if I'd run out of fuel, why I would have put down right there, but if I had any choice of a more promising spot, I was going to take it. There were some attractive areas, far more level, far less occupied by boulders, about a half-mile ahead or so, so that's where I went," Armstrong later remembered.

The landing spot Armstrong ultimately selected was 20,800 feet west and approximately 4,500 feet south of the original destination. Carefully monitoring computer flight data, Aldrin called out relevant numbers to his partner, as the lunar module neared the surface. Much to his relief, Armstrong found the LM easy to maneuver: "It settled down like a helicopter."

As the *Eagle's* fuel supply was rapidly disappearing, the stoic Armstrong seemed unfazed. In spite of his outward calm, the flight surgeons in Houston noted that Armstrong's heart rate had increased to 156 beats per minute during the final lunar descent. When the LM was 50 feet above the lunar surface, Mission Control radioed the *bingo fuel call,* meaning the *Eagle* had but 20 seconds to land.

With its fuel supply precariously low, the LM's landing sensors finally contacted the surface.

"Contact light," Aldrin relayed to Armstrong.

"Shutdown," Armstrong announced.

At 3:17:40 p.m., the lunar module touched down on the surface of the Moon.

"Houston, *Tranquility Base* here. The *Eagle* has landed," Armstrong announced to Mission Control and a worldwide television audience.

Aldrin later recalled his exact thoughts: "We had less than 20 seconds of fuel remaining, but we were on the Moon."

At Mission Control, the flight controllers and engineers in the *Trench* erupted in applause.

"Roger *Tranquility*, we copy you on the ground. You've got a bunch of guys about to turn blue. We're breathing again," Cap Com replied.

Armstrong and Aldrin shook hands and clapped one another on the back.

"There are lots of smiling faces in this room, and all over the world," Cap Com announced.

"There are two of them up here," Armstrong replied.

"And, don't forget the one in the command module," Michael Collins chimed in, orbiting high above the lunar surface.

"Whew, boy! Man on the Moon!" Walter Cronkite announced to *CBS* television viewers.

Far away from *Tranquility Base,* at Arlington National Cemetery, an anonymous visitor placed a small bouquet on the grave of John F. Kennedy, whose ambitious proposal, eight years earlier, heralded the *Apollo* program. A simple message was penned on the card attached to flowers: "Mr. President, the *Eagle* has landed."

CHAPTER 12

One small step

During space exploration, danger was a constant companion. Immediately after the *Eagle* landed on the Moon, Mission Control observed that the temperature in the descent engine fuel line had climbed to a dangerous level. NASA and *Grumman* engineers concluded that a "solid slug" of frozen fuel had trapped a small amount of overheated liquid in the line. If the temperature continued to rise, a catastrophic explosion was quite possible.

Two options were considered—aborting the mission, whereby the astronauts would immediately take off and leave the descent engine behind, or "burping" the engine, by quickly opening and closing the fuel line valve to relieve the mounting pressure. Neither choice was particularly appealing. Aborting the mission before the scheduled lunar excursion would be a major setback for the *Apollo* program. However, if the *Eagle* was not firmly planted on the lunar surface, the "burping" process could generate enough force to topple it over, stranding the astronauts on the Moon.

NASA officials faced a difficult choice, balancing mission goals with the safety of the flight crew. Suddenly, the pressure inside the fuel line began to drop, when the frozen fuel slug began melting. Fate had once again smiled on *Apollo 11*.

Soon after landing on the Moon, Buzz Aldrin conducted a pre-planned ritual of thanksgiving. A Communion kit had been prepared by Dean Woodruff, Pastor of Aldrin's Webster Presbyterian Church in Texas, allowing the astronaut to celebrate his blessings with bread and wine: "This is the LM pilot. I'd like to take this opportunity to ask every person listening in, whoever and wherever they may be, to pause for a moment and contemplate the events of the past few hours and to give thanks in his or her own way."

Aldrin's actions were not without controversy. Certain non-believers had vehemently protested the recitation of verses from the book of *Genesis* by the *Apollo 8* crew the previous Christmas Eve. Renowned atheist, Madalyn Murray, subsequently filed suit against NASA. The clergy and members of Webster Presbyterian Church, however, were honored—the church has since used Aldrin's chalice to celebrate an annual *Lunar Communion*, on the Sunday closest to July 20th.

Neil Armstrong, whose religious beliefs were a private matter, remained detached from his crewmate's ceremony: "He told me he planned a little celebratory Communion, and he asked if I had any problems with that, and I said, 'No, go right ahead.' I had plenty of things to keep busy with. I just let him do his own thing."

The *Apollo 11* astronauts were originally scheduled for a four-hour rest period prior to walking on the Moon. Far too excited to sleep, Armstrong and Aldrin received permission from Mission Control to move forward with the lunar excursion.

"Telling us to try to sleep before the *EVA* (*extra vehicular activity*) was like telling kids on Christmas morning they had to stay in bed until noon," Aldrin explained.

It took over four hours for the astronauts to complete their pre-EVA checklists. Conditions inside the lunar module were cramped, as Aldrin later recalled: "We felt like two fullbacks trying to change positions inside a Cub Scout pup tent."

Armstrong and Aldrin were already dressed in spandex and nylon *lunar underwear* equipped with 300 feet of plastic tubing to circulate water and maintain proper body temperature control.

Their external spacesuits, also known as extravehicular mobility units (EMU), constructed by *ILC Dover*, were designed to withstand the extreme lunar temperature fluctuations (+ 260 degrees to − 273 degrees Fahrenheit) and to protect against the impact of rock specks called *micrometeoroids*. At the same time, the spacesuit was designed to afford the astronauts with mobility while walking on the lunar surface. The seamstresses at *ILC Dover* had stitched, glued, and cemented together 22 layers of *Nomex, Neoprene*-coated nylon, *Beta* cloth (a fiberglass type material, coated with *Teflon*), and *Mylar* to create durable and functional spacesuits, costing $100,000.00 each.

After donning their bulky spacesuits, Armstrong and Aldrin disconnected themselves from *Eagle's* life support systems, becoming totally dependent on their portable life support system (PLSS) backpacks. The bulky units, developed by *Hamilton Standard Company*, provided the astronauts with a temperate atmosphere during their lunar excursion. The PLSS supplied oxygen, maintained appropriate body pressure, supplied water to keep the astronauts' bodies climate controlled, and housed communication equipment. A separate, smaller pack, worn on their chests, contained a pump for the water-cooling system, a fan for oxygen circulation, a communications switch, and in Armstrong's case, a camera mount.

The astronauts' helmets were equipped with tinted visors to ward off the Sun's ultraviolet rays; a necessity, since the Moon has no protective atmospheric layer of its own. Armstrong and Aldrin wore special boots to promote traction on the yet unknown texture of the lunar surface. The combined weight of the spacesuit and PLSS was 180 pounds, but with lunar gravitational forces less than 1/6th of the Earth's, the extra load was equivalent to only 30 pounds.

Before stepping foot on the lunar surface, the astronauts vented oxygen from the LM's cabin. Once the cabin was depressurized and the hatch opened, seven hours after landing, Commander Neil Armstrong was ready to make history.

Aldrin helped his crewmate, who was encumbered by his bulky space suit and PLSS, negotiate passage through the narrow hatch. On his hands and knees, Armstrong backed his way out the hatch onto the *porch,* a small platform at the top of the descent ladder.

As he began to step backwards down the ladder, Armstrong pulled a lanyard, releasing the modularized equipment stowage assembly (MESA)—a workbench and storage area at the base of the lunar module. The MESA housed a black and white television camera aimed at the foot of the ladder, which was programed to record Armstrong's historic first steps. At the bottom of the ladder, Armstrong jumped three feet down to the footpad, located just inches above the lunar surface.

"I'm at the foot of the ladder. The LM footpads are depressed in the surface about one or two inches," Armstrong reported, "The surface appears to be very, very fine grained, as you get close to it. It's almost like powder."

As 500,000,000 people, $1/15^{th}$ of the world's population, watched on television, Armstrong was poised to make history: "I'm going to step off the LM now..."

At 9:56:20 p.m., Neil Armstrong stepped onto the surface of the Moon, announcing to the world: "That's one small step for man, one giant leap for mankind."

Armstrong, who had not shared his planned statement in advance, later recalled the sentence did not come out exactly as he had hoped. In the excitement of the moment, he had left out one word, having planned to say: "That's one small step for *a* man, one giant leap for mankind." Armstrong, alone, was aware of the omission, and his prosaic description of the historic moment seemed most fitting.

"Armstrong is on the Moon. Neil Armstrong, 38-year-old American, standing on the surface of the Moon!" Walter Cronkite exclaimed to *CBS* viewers, as the camera mounted on the MESA delivered a clear image of the monumental first steps.

"Isn't this something? 240,000 miles out there, and we're seeing this!" Cronkite excitedly reported.

Armstrong's boots lightly penetrated the lunar soil: "The surface is fine and powdery...I can see the footprints of my boots."

Armstrong immediately inspected the area at the base of lunar module: "The descent engine did not leave a crater of any size. It has about one-foot clearance on the ground. We're essentially on a very level place, here," he reported.

Before exploring his new environment, Armstrong used his contingency sampler to scoop up a small amount of lunar soil, which he placed in a Teflon bag and then stored in the pocket on one leg of his space suit. The hastily gathered contingency sample would be available if the *Apollo 11* mission was suddenly aborted, before the crew could gather more soil and rocks.

Armstrong began to walk away from the lunar module, adjusting his gait to match the reduced gravity and accommodate the bulkiness of his spacesuit. With its diameter smaller than Earth's, the Moon's planetoid curve was more visible, and Armstrong had to watch where he was walking, keeping his eyes several steps ahead, to keep from falling. After establishing his "lunar legs," the mission commander ventured as far as 60 yards away from the lunar module, while examining the neighboring *East Crater.*

Armstrong described the lunar topography: "It has a stark beauty of its own. It's much like the high desert of the United States."

Buzz Aldrin waited patiently inside the lunar module, biding his time and taking repeated photographs of the lunar surface. Nineteen minutes after Armstrong's descent, it was Aldrin's turn.

"Okay. Are you ready for me to come out?" Aldrin radioed his crewmate.

"All set. Okay. You saw what difficulties I was having (clearing the hatch). I'll try to watch your PLSS from underneath here," Armstrong replied.

Standing near the base of the lunar module, Armstrong carefully photographed his crewmate's painstaking descent. Once he was on the porch, Aldrin paused: "Okay. Now, I want to go back up and partially close the hatch, making sure not to lock it on my way out."

"A pretty good thought," Armstrong chuckled.

111

"That's our home for the next couple of hours, and we want to take care of it," Aldrin emphasized; an important point, as outside of the hatch did not have a handle, and if the door had sealed shut, the astronauts would have been stranded on the lunar surface.

Armstrong watched Aldrin gradually back down the ladder: "You've got three more steps and then a long one."

After Buzz Aldrin's feet touched the lunar surface, he shared his observations with the world: "Beautiful view."

"Isn't that something? Magnificent sight out here," Armstrong replied.

"Magnificent desolation," Aldrin spontaneously exclaimed.

Armstrong placed his gloved hand on Aldrin's shoulder: "Isn't it fun?"

Aldrin carefully surveyed the barren terrain: "I felt buoyant and full of goose pimples when I stepped down on the surface. I immediately looked down at my feet, and became intrigued with the peculiar properties of lunar dust. If one kicks sand on a beach, it scatters in numerous directions, with some grains traveling farther than others. On the Moon, dust travels exactly and precisely as it goes in various directions, and every grain of it lands nearly the same distance away."

The astronauts spied Earth in the distant sky. With a reflective power four times greater than the Moon, and a reflective surface area 13 times as large, the home planet was a majestic sight.

Aldrin later recalled the scenic vista: "The shadows and sky were as black as the blackest velvet I had ever seen." He also practiced his lunar gait: "One of my tests was to jog away from the LM to see how maneuverable an astronaut was on the surface. I remembered what Isaac Newton had taught us two centuries before—mass and weight are not the same. I weighed only 60 pounds, but my mass was the same as it was on Earth. Inertia was a problem. I had to plan ahead several steps to bring myself to a stop or turn, without falling."

Possessing little time for reflection, Armstrong and Aldrin quickly set to work completing their numerous assigned tasks, retrieving the necessary equipment from the storage bins in the

MESA. As Aldrin fed cable to him from the base of the lunar module, Armstrong set up a color television camera 50 feet away.

Most of the astronauts' activity occurred within 100 feet of the LM. By the end of the lunar excursion, the pair had collected 48 pounds of rock and soil. Hammering their lunar rocks core sampler tube eight to nine inches into the Moon's surface, Armstrong and Aldrin were able to retrieve subterranean samples to go along with their growing above ground rock and soil collection. The astronauts also deployed the passive seismic experiment package (PSEP), designed to monitor the intensity of *Moonquakes* and measure the seismographic impact of meteor strikes on the lunar surface. A laser-ranging retro reflector (LRRR) was also erected; the two by two feet mirror reflected laser beams from Earth, allowing scientists to calculate the exact distance from Earth to the Moon. The pair also conducted a solar wind composition (SWC) experiment, whereby a thin layer of aluminum foil was used to entrap the noble gases, like helium, neon, argon, krypton, and xenon, all of which were active components of the solar wind. The foil sheet was ultimately transported back to Earth for detailed study.

At 10:47 p.m., Armstrong and Aldrin interrupted their work to receive a special call, patched through by Mission Control: "Neil and Buzz, the President of the United States is in his office now, and would like say a few words to you. Over."

"That would be an honor," Armstrong replied.

"Go ahead, Mr. President. This is Houston. Out," Cap Com announced.

"Neil and Buzz, I am talking by telephone from the Oval Room at the White House, and this certainly has to be the most historic telephone call ever made from the White House. I just can't tell you how proud we all are of what you have done for every American. This has to be the proudest day of our lives. And, for people all over the world, I am sure they, too, join with Americans in recognizing what an immense feat this is. Because of what you have done, the heavens have become part of man's world. And, as you talk to us from the *Sea of Tranquility*, it inspires us to redouble our efforts to bring peace and tranquility to Earth. For one priceless moment in the whole history of man, all people on this Earth are truly one—one in their pride in what you have done, and one in our prayers that you will return safely to Earth."

"Thank you, Mr. President. It's a great honor and privilege for us to be representing not only the United States, but men of peace of all nations, and with interest and curiosity, and a vision for the future. It's an honor for us to be able to participate today," Armstrong replied.

In short order, the astronauts resumed their work on the lunar surface, consulting checklists attached to the sleeves of their space-suits. Using pencils and graph paper, engineers at Mission Control monitored oxygen levels in each astronaut's PLSS. The life support packs performed flawlessly, and Armstrong and Aldrin were given permission to extend their lunar excursion by a quarter of an hour.

"We've been looking at your consumables—we'd like to extend the duration of the EVA one-five minutes from nominal," Cap Com radioed.

At one point, Aldrin paused briefly to study his home planet in the distant horizon: "I looked high above the dome of the LM. Earth hung in the black sky, a disk cut in half by the day-night terminator. It was mostly blue, with swirling white clouds, and I could make out a brown land mass—North Africa and the Middle East."

Sixty miles above the lunar surface, Michael Collins was perhaps the loneliest man in the universe. Forty-eight minutes out of every two hours, the CSM traveled to the *dark side* of the Moon, which placed Collins outside of radio contact with Mission Control and his crewmates below.

"I knew I was alone in a way that no Earthling has ever been before," Collins remembered.

When Collins passed over the *Sea of Tranquility*, he used his sextant, a lunar area map (LAM-20) and check-off grids to try and locate the *Eagle*. Neither Collins nor Mission Control knew the exact coordinates of the revised landing site, and the command module pilot was unable to pinpoint the location of his crewmates on the surface.

Prior to the historic lunar mission, NASA's Chief of Photography, Richard Underwood, stressed to Armstrong and Aldrin the importance of quality photography: "The key to immortality is solely in the quality of your photographs. If your photographs are great—they'll live forever. If someone really wants to know you went, they'll see your pictures." Underwood taught the astronauts how to "shoot from the hip" with their *Hasselblad* still cameras, explaining the impracticality of using the view finders while wearing bulky spacesuits and helmets with darkened visors. Prior to the *Apollo 11* launch, both astronauts practiced zero-gravity photography inside a parabola-flying *KC-135* aircraft.

The *Apollo 11* crew carried with them three separate 70-millimeter *Hasselblad* super wide-angle cameras. Armstrong and Aldrin each utilized a camera while on the lunar surface, while a third *Hasselblad* remained in the CSM with Collins.

Perhaps the most unforgettable still shot was taken by Neil Armstrong. In this photograph, both Armstrong and the lunar module can be seen in the reflection from Aldrin's visor. When asked later about the historic photograph, Aldrin jokingly replied: "I have only three words—location, location, location!"

Another timeless picture featured Aldrin saluting an American flag the astronauts had mounted on the lunar surface. The flag, three by five feet, was attached to a pole, eight-feet-long, with a horizontal wire to hold it in place—the bent wire created the illusion of the flag waving in the windless atmosphere. Armstrong and Aldrin worked hard to set up this photo opportunity, but the absence of air or moisture in the lunar soil made it difficult for the astronauts to firmly insert the hollow flagpole into the Moon's surface.

Of the roughly 100 color photographs taken on the surface of the Moon, only five featured Neil Armstrong. While focusing on other areas, Aldrin rarely captured his crewmate in the camera lens. While some of Aldrin's critics have suggested his actions were deliberate pay back for not being chosen as the first man to walk on the Moon, the *Apollo 11* commander was nonplussed: "We didn't spend any time worrying about who took what pictures...I have always said that Buzz was the far more photogenic of the crew." Aldrin offered a simpler, non-sinister explanation—Armstrong had the lone spacesuit camera mount, so it was logical for him (Armstrong) to shoot the majority of the lunar surface photographs.

In addition to the black and white television camera mounted on the base of the lunar module, which had captured Neil Armstrong's first steps, the astronauts also employed a color camera during their lunar excursion; both television cameras were manufactured by *Westinghouse*. The second camera, resting on a tripod, provided a panoramic view of the area surrounding the lunar module.

In order for television viewers to witness the live broadcast, the cameras on the Moon had to relay images to three giant antennae on Earth, located in Australia, Spain, and Nevada. The receiving stations sent the lunar images, via satellite, to Mission Control in Houston, where they were then relayed to the three major television networks in New York City, and subsequently transmitted to television sets around the world. This nearly instantaneous, yet laborious technological feat required the coordinated efforts of thousands of technicians all over the world.

Based on the rotational alignment of the Earth and Moon on that particular night, the Parkes radio telescope in Australia was positioned to receive the clearest signal. Located in the middle of a pasture surrounded by grazing sheep, the Parkes antennae broadcast the majority of the 2.5-hour lunar excursion, amidst a fierce storm, complicated by wind gusts of up to 70 miles per hour. The brave men and women who worked at the receiving station risked their lives by standing on top, inside, and below the giant satellite dish, which could have easily collapsed during the violent squalls.

Neil Armstrong and Buzz Aldrin left a lasting imprint on the lunar surface. On the landing gear of the *Eagle*, which would remain on the Moon after the lunar module ascended, the astronauts unveiled a plaque: "Here men came from the planet Earth first set foot on the Moon. July 1969, A.D. We came in peace for all mankind." The marker was signed by all three *Apollo 11* astronauts and President Nixon. In addition, a bag was left on the lunar surface containing a variety of objects: a gold replica of an olive branch, signifying peace; a silicone disc, containing goodwill messages from Presidents Eisenhower, Kennedy, Johnson, and Nixon, as well as 73 other world leaders; an *Apollo 1* patch, honoring deceased astronauts, Gus Grissom, Ed White, and Roger Chafee; a roster of the existing congressional leadership; a compilation of the members of the four House and Senate Committees responsible for NASA legislation; a list of the present and past NASA management leaders; and Soviet medals honoring deceased cosmonauts, Vladimir Komarov and Yuri Gagarin.

Armstrong and Aldrin were allowed to transport personal items to the Moon and back. Armstrong carried a number of *Apollo 11* cloth patches, gold olive branch pins for his wife and mother, and his Purdue University college fraternity pin. Aldrin brought with him several pieces of jewelry for his wife and other family members, in addition to the vial and chalice used during his lunar Communion.

Near the conclusion of their lunar excursion, Armstrong and Aldrin loaded 48 pounds of Moon rock and soil aboard the lunar module. The lunar equipment conveyor, a pulley-type device, was used to hoist the vacuum-sealed, flameproof, metal boxes containing the precious geological samples into the LM.

Two hours and 19 minutes after he stepped on the surface of the Moon, Buzz Aldrin was the first to re-enter the lunar module, followed 33 minutes later by Armstrong. That same day, *Luna 15* crashed into the lunar surface, ending the Soviet Union's quest to retrieve Moon rocks and soil samples and return to Earth ahead of *Apollo 11*.

The Space Race was officially over.

CHAPTER 13
Hot diggety dog!

After their history-making walk on the Moon, Neil Armstrong and Buzz Aldrin undertook a series of housekeeping chores before closing the lunar module's hatch. To lessen the *Eagle's* weight and conserve space, several items of "trash" were dumped on the lunar surface, including the astronaut's portable life system backpacks and boots, both *Hasselblad* cameras, empty food packets, and urine/fecal containment bags.

After securing the hatch and re-establishing suitable cabin pressure, the astronauts were able to take off their dusty space suits. In zero gravity, small grains of lunar soil floated throughout the cabin. Armstrong thought the Moon dust smelled like "wet ashes," while Aldrin likened the odor to "gunpowder or the smell in the air after a firecracker has gone off."

Before discarding their cameras, the astronauts took memorable photographs of each other wearing their nylon jumpsuits and *Snoopy caps* (cloth head covers with built in radio headphones). For the briefest of moments, Armstrong's innate stoicism gave way to a boyish grin.

After a meal of cocktail sausages and fruit punch, the astronauts were scheduled for a rest period. In the tight quarters, Aldrin was forced to sleep on the cockpit floor, while Armstrong settled atop the ascent engine's 30-inch, circular cover, held in place by a sling. As a precaution against excessive exposure to drifting particles of Moon dust, the astronauts were instructed to wear their bulky helmets and gloves while sleeping. The chilly temperature (61 degrees F), noisy glycol and water pumps, and bright light creeping through the cockpit window and sextant made sleep difficult. Not surprisingly, both men remained in a heightened state of excitement, contributing to what Aldrin remembered as a "fitful state of drowsiness."

After seven hours of restless sleep and a quick breakfast, the astronauts began preparing the lunar module for departure. The lunar ascent was fraught with peril—if the engine failed, Armstrong and Aldrin had only a 24-hour supply of life-sustaining oxygen. Once again forced to cast fear aside, the astronauts used the lunar module's telescope to sight stars and calculate the appropriate alignment for lunar ascent.

Orbiting high above the lunar surface, Michael Collins started his day early. Prior to docking and rendezvous with *Eagle,* the command module pilot had a checklist of chores, including 850 separate computer keystrokes. Likening his emotional state to that of a "nervous bride," Collins' worst fears would be realized if the lunar ascent failed—he would be forced to leave his doomed crewmates on the Moon.

Compared to most other technological aspects of the *Apollo 11* mission, the lunar module's lunar ascent engine was rather simple in design. Manufactured by *Rocketdyne* and *Bell Aerosystems,* the engine had only four moving parts, but was capable of generating 3,500 pounds of thrust, and could accelerate from zero to 3,000 miles per hour within two minutes. When the engine rockets fired, a guillotine would separate the LM into two separate pieces. The upper, ascent stage would blast into orbit, while the lower section would remain on the Moon permanently. Prior to their lunar lift-off, the astronauts encountered a serious problem. The night before, while preparing for his forthcoming

Moon walk, Aldrin's bulky PLSS had inadvertently broken the circuit breaker responsible for firing the LM's ascent engine. A resourceful Aldrin was forced to improvise, using a felt tip pen as substitute starter switch.

"I don't suppose we've been this nervous since back in the early days of Mercury," Walter Cronkite reminded his captive television audience.

At 12:55 p.m., Mission Control radioed the astronauts: "Roger, *Eagle*. You're clear for takeoff."

"Roger. Understand we're number one on the runway," Armstrong quipped.

As NASA flight controllers head their breath, yet again, Buzz Aldrin's jury-rigged switch successfully activated the ascent engine, and *Eagle* blasted away from the *Sea of Tranquility*, completing a 21-hour, 37-minute visit to the Moon. During lift-off, Aldrin noted, much to his chagrin, the flag pole bearing the Stars and Stripes, which had been precariously mounted on the lunar surface, toppled over.

"Very smooth, a very quiet ride," Aldrin notified Mission Control, as the lunar module raced skyward at the rate of 30 feet per second.

Unlike the descent phase, when the astronauts were preoccupied with locating a landing site, they were now able to enjoy the view, identifying specific topographical landmarks.

In the event the LM was unable to dock with the CSM, Aldrin and Armstrong would have to exit the lunar module and space walk to the mother ship, where Collins would open the capsule hatch and let them inside. With his many and varied experiences, Neil Armstrong had never actually attempted a spacewalk.

It took 3 hours and 40 minutes for *Eagle* to establish orbital docking alignment with *Columbia,* 69 miles above the lunar surface. At 4:38 p.m., Armstrong and Collins piloted their respective spacecraft into position, and successfully executed the exacting docking maneuver. For the next two hours, Armstrong and Aldrin remained in the lunar module, disabling its systems.

When Michael Collins finally opened the tunnel hatch, he was both elated and relieved to eyeball his fellow astronauts. Grasping Aldrin's temple, the command module pilot was tempted to kiss his crewmate's balding forehead, but instead, settled for firm handshakes with both men.

After transferring the lunar rock samples and other equipment from the LM into the CSM, the *Apollo 11* crew used a special vacuum cleaner to remove lunar dust particles that had drifted inside *Columbia* through the open passageway.

At 6:42 p.m., *Eagle* was jettisoned into lunar orbit, where it would remain for several months, before crashing onto the Moon's surface. Collins, delighted to have his crewmates back safe and sound, was grateful to see the lunar module drift away, but intuitively sensed the moods of his travel companions: "Neil and Buzz, on the other hand, seemed genuinely sad—old 'Eagle' had served them well and deserved a formal, or at least, a dignified burial."

At Studio 41 on West 57th Street in Manhattan, *CBS News* was winding up 32 hours of continuous coverage of the lunar mission. Walter Cronkite's broadcast desk, which had been raised 24 feet above the studio floor, featured a mural of the Milky Way as a celestial backdrop. Alongside Cronkite and his guest analyst, *Mercury 7* astronaut Wally Schirra, globes and a *Rand McNally* model of the Moon shared center stage. Cronkite, who during one stretch, spent 17.5 consecutive hours on the air, had been emotional at times; his eyes filled with tears when *Eagle* landed on the lunar surface. When the lunar module and CSM docked, successfully completing the lunar ascent phase of the mission, the seemingly tireless news anchor giddily exclaimed: "Hot diggety dog!"

CBS and Cronkite were riding high. Ninety-four percent of all American homes had tuned into to watch the astronauts walk on the Moon—out of that viewership, *CBS* won a 45 percent share compared to *NBC's* 34 percent (*ABC* was a distant third, with 16 percent).

As the marathon broadcast neared its conclusion, Cronkite succinctly and melodically summarized the monumental achievement:

"Man has finally visited the Moon after all the ages of waiting and waiting. Two Americans, with the alliterative names of Armstrong and Aldrin, have spent just under a full Earth day on the Moon. They picked at it and sampled it, and they deployed experiments on it, and they packed away some of it to pack with them and bring home."

CHAPTER 14

We got you coming home

On Monday night, July 21, 1969, Michael Collins fired *Columbia's* service propulsion engines for 2.5 minutes, accelerating the spacecraft's speed to 6,188 miles per hour. Like so many other aspects of the *Apollo 11* mission, the engine burn was fraught with danger. If the spacecraft's engines failed to respond, the astronauts would be stranded in lunar orbit. After accelerating to an escape velocity of 2,238 miles per hour, the CSM overcame the gravitational pull of the Moon and completed the process of *trans-Earth injection.*

"We got you coming home," Mission Control announced to the crew.

The return trip to Earth required two and one-half days, and during that time, only one course correction engine burn was required. As *Columbia* sped homeward, Collins reflected how it was "nice to sit here and watch the Earth getting larger and larger, and Moon getting smaller and smaller."

The Earth-bound astronauts were informed by Mission Control that the recently launched unmanned Russian probe, *Luna 15*, had crashed on the Moon, yet again stymieing the Soviet lunar exploration program. The news coverage, however, was dominated by the *Apollo 11* mission. The front page of the July 21st issue of the

THE EAGLE HAS LANDED

Washington Post read: THE EAGLE HAS LANDED—TWO MEN WALK ON THE MOON. The *New York Times* featured a similar headline: MAN WALKS ON MOON—ASTRONAUTS LAND ON PLAIN AFTER STEERING PAST CRATER. Predictably, the Soviet Union downplayed the historic event, with *Pravda* burying the story in its back pages.

During their trip home, Armstrong, Aldrin, and Collins began preparing for their newfound roles as American heroes. In the months to follow, the trio would be universally acclaimed and their names and faces etched in history. Even before they returned to Earth, the astronauts undertook tasks to commemorate their historic mission. Using a cancellation stamp, the Earth-bound voyagers prepared a new 10-cent postage stamp, featuring the image of an astronaut on the Moon.

When *Columbia* was 174,000 miles from home, Earth's gravitational pull overtook the opposing lunar force, further accelerating the spacecraft. On the eve of splashdown, the astronauts delivered their last daily television broadcast. Michael Collins spent a portion of his allotted broadcast time thanking the people behind the scenes: "This trip of ours to the Moon may have looked simple or easy. I'd like to assure you that has not been the case. The *Saturn V* rocket which put us in orbit is an incredibly complicated piece of machinery, every piece of which worked flawlessly."

"This operation is somewhat like the periscope of a submarine. All you see is the three of us, but beneath the surface are thousands of others, and to all of those, I would like to say, 'Thank your very much,'" Collins concluded.

Buzz Aldrin discussed the future of space exploration: "We accepted the challenge of going to the Moon—the acceptance of this challenge was inevitable. The relative ease with which we carried out our mission, I believe, it is a tribute to the timeliness of that acceptance. Today, I feel we're really capable of accepting expanded roles in the exploration of space."

Mission commander Neil Armstrong spoke last, expressing appreciation to the thousands of men and women who made their mission an unqualified success: "We would like to give special thanks to those Americans who built those spacecraft—who did the construction, design, the tests, and put their hearts and all their abilities into those craft. To those people, tonight, we give special thanks to you. And, to all other people who are listening, and watching tonight, God bless you. Good night from *Apollo 11*."

CHAPTER 15
Everyone okay inside

A t 11:22 a.m., on Thursday July 24, 1969, the *Apollo 11* crew jettisoned the spacecraft's service module, 400,000 feet above the Earth's surface. The 11,000-pound command module was now all that remained of the original 6,000,000-pound launch vehicle.

"It's been a champ," Michael Collins reminisced, watching the second to last component drift away into space.

After the service module was discarded, Collins turned the command module completely around, so the blunt end, protected by its heat shield, would lead the way during passage through Earth's uppermost atmosphere. Traveling at a speed of 25,000 miles per hour, the spacecraft's angle of re-entry was critical. A miscalculation would cause the capsule to either *bounce off* Earth, sending the astronauts on a perpetual journey into outer space, or cause it to incinerate in the atmosphere. The 40-mile-wide re-entry corridor, -6.48 degrees, was a narrow target for the command module pilot.

At 11:35 a.m., high above the northeastern coast of Australia, *Columbia* made a flawless re-entry, beginning the final leg of its historic journey. As expected, the astronauts encountered a rough ride, accelerating from zero gravity to a 6G force. Outside the capsule, temperatures soared to 5,000 degrees (F).

The ablative heat shield was the capsule's only protection against incineration. Developed by *Avco,* the shield consisted of 4,000 cells, interwoven to form a protective honeycomb. The phenolic epoxy resin (reinforced plastic) was designed to melt away when exposed to the intense heat of re-entry, creating a protective cover around the blunt end of the spacecraft.

As *Apollo 11* sped through Earth's atmosphere at 36,000 feet per second, the heat shield turned a flaming orange-red color. During the height of re-entry, radio waves could not penetrate the fiery cloud surrounding the capsule. The eerie silence lasted for four minutes, as the world anxiously awaited word from the homebound astronauts.

When *Columbia* emerged from the clouds high above the Pacific Ocean, NASA officials and millions of television viewers breathed a sigh of relief. At 24,000 feet, two drogue parachutes stabilized the capsule in a vertical position, decelerating it enough for the main chutes to be effective. Three ringtail chutes, 83-feet in diameter, deployed at 10,000 feet, slowing the spacecraft to a safe landing speed.

Due to unfavorable weather conditions, the splash down site had been moved 215 miles down range from its original location. The aircraft carrier, *USS Hornet,* was 13 miles away from the target zone, where helicopters and recovery teams were poised for action.

"*11,* this is *Hornet.* What's your error of splashdown, and condition of crew?" the recovery team coordinator inquired.

"The condition of crew is excellent. We're 4,000 to 3,500 feet, on the way down," Neil Armstrong replied.

The spacecraft's revised landing spot was 940 nautical miles southwest of Honolulu and 1,440 nautical miles east of Wake Island—13 degrees, 19 minutes North and 169 degrees, 9 minutes West. At 11:49 a.m., *Columbia* splashed down in the Pacific Ocean, 8 days, 3 hours, 18 minutes, and 30 seconds after lift-off. Neil Armstrong acknowledged the successful landing: "Everyone okay inside. Awaiting swimmers."

At Mission Control, applause erupted in the *Trench.* The flight controllers exchanged handshakes and raised their fists in triumph. While tiny American flags were excitedly waved, a hand-ful of exhausted flight controllers lit victory cigars.

After landing in the unsettling Pacific waters, the capsule im-mediately flipped over into the stable two position, leaving the crew dangling upside down in their cockpit seats. The automatic deployment of *Columbia's* airbags soon righted the spacecraft into the stable one position. The astronauts took a second motion sick-ness pill, having already swallowed one prior to re-entry, and were better able to tolerate the choppy seas, while awaiting arrival of the recovery team.

At 12:20 p.m., Navy swimmers arrived and inflated a flotation collar around the base of the capsule to improve stability. The hatch was briefly opened, and a recovery team diver hastily tossed three biological containment garments (BIGS) inside the capsule. Almost immediately after returning to Earth, the *Apollo 11* crew was forced to begin the isolation phase of their mission; NASA's medical epidemiologists were uncertain if pathogenic biological organisms dwelled on the Moon, and were determined to prevent an unprecedented and potentially untreatable epidemic.

After spending eight days in space, the astronauts felt a bit dizzy and noted slight swelling in their feet and legs as they ad-justed to the force of gravity, but had no difficulty donning their BIGS. Exiting the open hatch door, Armstrong, Aldrin, and Collins jumped into the adjacent inflatable life raft, where they spent several minutes spraying and wiping one other with liquid disinfectant.

One by one, the astronauts were lifted by a basket into the re-covery helicopter hovering overhead. A hero's welcome awaited them.

CHAPTER 16

The greatest week in the history of the world, since Creation

Confined within their stifling biological contamination suits, the astronauts were unable to speak to each other or the recovery crew as they were taken by helicopter to the *USS Hornet.* Michael Collins tried a couple of deep knee bends to exercise his gravity-deprived body, but quickly discovered extraneous movements made him feel more uncomfortable in the claustrophobic isolation garment.

After landing on the deck of the aircraft carrier, the astronauts were immediately transferred to the mobile quarantine facility (MQF), which Collins referred to as "a gloried trailer without wheels." The trailer was divided into three sections—a lounge area, galley, and sleep/bath area. Armstrong, Aldrin, and Collins were joined in quarantine by a NASA flight surgeon and a mechanical engineer, the latter of whom was responsible for cooking and housekeeping chores, as well as sterilization of the lunar rock samples.

The astronauts were finally allowed to remove their suffocating contamination suits, and for the first time in eight days, were able to take a shower. The freshly scrubbed trio was then led to the MQF's lounge area, where a glass window separated them from President Richard Nixon, who had come aboard the *Hornet* to personally greet the heroes. Nixon praised the astronauts for their courage and skill, hailing the *Apollo 11* mission as "the greatest week in the history of the world, since Creation."

The *Apollo 11* crew spent two nights aboard the *USS Hornet*, while the aircraft carrier cruised to Hawaii. At Pearl Harbor, the MQF was loaded on a flat bed truck, and the astronauts were paraded through the streets of Honolulu, lined with cheering crowds. At Hickam Air Force Base, the trailer was loaded onto a *C-141* transport plane and flown to Ellington Air Force Base in Houston. Thousands of gleeful Texans applauded all along the route from the air base to Mission Control.

At the Manned Space Flight Center, Armstrong, Aldrin, and Collins departed the trailer and entered the lunar receiving laboratory (LRL), a much more spacious facility with individual, private quarters. The astronauts were joined in the LRL by cooks, housekeepers, and flight surgeons. Once anyone entered the quarantine area, they would not be allowed to leave until the *Apollo 11* astronauts were released. A whimsical sign was erected over the entrance to the LRL: "Please don't feed the animals."

The *Apollo 11* crew remained in active quarantine for three weeks. During their confinement in the LRL, the trio underwent medical examinations and debriefings, and spent hours writing detailed reports about their lunar mission. In typical bureaucratic fashion, each astronaut was asked to submit a personal voucher for travel-related expenses—Neil Armstrong was ultimately reimbursed by the federal government, in the amount of $49.10. They were also required to fill out a customs declaration form, acknowledging the transport of Moon rock and soil samples into the United States, with a port of entry in Hawaii.

During the quarantine period, NASA scientists performed a variety of tests to determine if infectious microorganism had accompanied the astronauts from the Moon to Earth. A group of germ-free mice were exposed to the astronauts and their lunar surface equipment. Soil and rock samples from the Moon were placed in a culture media to monitor the potential growth and development of pathogens. Human and animal culture cells, embryos, 33 species of plants and seedlings, and a variety of animals, including fish, birds, oysters, shrimp, houseflies, planarian, paramecia, and euglena, were also exposed to lunar material. When none of the life forms contracted previously unrecognized infectious diseases, fears of contamination with *Moon bugs* were temporarily dispelled.

NASA officials were eager to examine the hundreds of photographs taken by Armstrong and Aldrin while on the lunar surface, but fears of biological contamination rendered immediate picture-viewing difficult. NASA Chief of Photography, Richard Underwood, proposed that the film remain undeveloped until the quarantine period was complete. Underwood was quickly overruled by NASA administrators, and ordered to develop a method to decontaminate the film, without damaging or destroying the irreplaceable photographs. Consequently, the film rolls were placed in stainless steel containers and exposed to gaseous ethylene oxide, designed to exterminate potential lunar pathogens. As hoped, the still photography was magnificent, and many of those images now grace the pages of history books.

At 9:00 p.m. on August 13, 1969, three weeks after splash down, the *Apollo 11* crew exited the quarantine facility. Over the next several weeks, the conquering heroes were featured guests at numerous banquets and receptions. Armstrong, Aldrin, and Collins were flown aboard *Air Force Two* to New York City, Chicago, and Los Angeles, where ticker tape parades were held in their honor. In Los Angeles, an official State Dinner honoring the astronauts was hosted by President Nixon and Vice-President Spiro Agnew. Among the distinguished guests attending the black tie affair were 44 Governors, the Chief Justice of the Supreme Court, and Ambassadors from 83 foreign nations.

President Nixon formally recognized the historic achievements of the *Apollo 11* crew: "It has been my privilege in the White House, and also in other world capitals, to propose toasts to many distinguished people, to Emperors, to Kings, to Presidents, to Prime Ministers, and yes, to a Duke, and tonight, this is the highest privilege I could have, to propose a toast to America's astronauts."

On August 16th, 300,000 people jammed the streets of Houston for a parade honoring the *Apollo 11* crew. That night, a crowd of 45,000 gathered in the Astrodome to celebrate the triumphant lunar mission. Frank Sinatra was among the featured entertainers, serenading the joyous crowd with *Fly Me to the Moon.*

The *Apollo 11* crew soon departed on a six-continent *Giant Leap Tour,* otherwise known as *Operation Giant Step.* Greeted with international acclaim, the astronauts and their spouses traveled to 23 countries over the course of 45 days.

Amidst the post-mission celebration, the astronauts occasionally encountered unpleasantness. At Marquette University, the *Apollo 11* crew was pelted with eggs and tomatoes by an angry mob of Vietnam War protestors.

On September 16, 1969, Armstrong, Aldrin, and Collins addressed a joint session of Congress. The astronauts presented the Senators and Congressmen with a pair of American flags that had traveled to the Moon and back—one each for the House of Representatives and the Senate.

The numerous accolades received by the *Apollo 11* astronauts were justifiable, etching their names in the annals of history. Neil Armstrong, Buzz Aldrin, and Michael Collins seemed largely unfazed by the publicity, and would remain forever grateful for the opportunity afforded to them. The *Apollo 11* crew viewed their historical achievement as simply a call to duty.

Perhaps the single best tribute came from the pen of Michael Collins. While still in quarantine aboard the *USS Hornet,* Collins made a secret visit to the command module. On the capsule's cockpit wall, he wrote: "Spacecraft 107—alias *Apollo 11*—alias *Columbia.* The best ship to come down the line. God Bless her. Michael Collins, CMP."

EPILOGUE

On November 19, 1969, four months after Neil Armstrong became the first man to step foot on the Moon, *Apollo 12's* lunar module touched down in the *Ocean of Storms*, only 600 feet from the unmanned *Surveyor* probe that had landed there in 1967. Astronauts Alan Bean and Pete Conrad spent over 31 hours on the lunar surface.

The *Apollo 12* mission was barely underway, when complications arose. Just 36 seconds after lift-off, at an altitude of 1,859 meters, the *Saturn V* rocket was struck by lightning. Fifty-two seconds later, lightning struck the rocket a second time. The spacecraft's electronic systems immediately went haywire, leaving the crew in total darkness, before the back-up system restored power.

On April 11, 1970, *Apollo 13* was launched from Cape Canaveral. After traveling some 200,000 miles from Earth, mission commander James Lovell radioed Mission Control with the now famous words: "Okay, Houston. We have a problem."

A ruptured oxygen tank in the service module forced cancellation of the lunar landing and threatened the lives of the crew. Lovell and his crewmates, John Swigert and Fred Haise, had to conserve electricity and water, utilizing the lunar module's power and oxygen supply during their perilous, but ultimately successful swing around the Moon and return home.

On February 5, 1971, the *Apollo 14* lunar module landed in the *Frau Mauro* lunar highlands. Forty-seven-year-old Alan Shepard, America's first space voyager, served as mission commander, having returned to active duty following surgery to correct vertigo—a medical problem that had grounded him for nearly 10 years. Shepard and fellow astronaut Ed Mitchell became the fifth and sixth men to walk on the Moon. The image of Shepard hitting a golf ball on the lunar surface with a modified six iron is a permanent fixture in *Apollo* lore.

Apollo 15's LM landed on the Moon on July 30, 1971. The lunar rover, a battery-powered dune buggy-type vehicle, folded and stored inside the base of the LM, was used for the first time during this mission, allowing the astronauts to travel greater distances from the landing site. During their lunar excursions, spread out over three days, astronauts David Scott and Jim Irwin launched a small satellite into lunar orbit, providing NASA scientists with a new means of collecting data about the Moon. The *Apollo 15* astronauts were the first crew to forego the post flight quarantine; repeated tests had established that there were no infectious *Moon bugs.*

On April, 20 1972, the *Apollo 16* lunar module landed on the Moon. Astronauts Charlie Duke and John Young set up an observatory on the lunar surface, providing NASA scientists with a bird's eye view of the Milky Way and beyond. During their three-day-stay on the Moon, Duke and Young collected 208.3 pounds of rocks and soil samples.

The sixth and final manned lunar landing occurred on December 11, 1972. The *Apollo 17* mission lasted for 12 days, during which time astronauts Gene Cernan and Harrison Schmitt collected 240 pounds of geological specimens.

Apollo missions *18, 19,* and *20* were cancelled due to NASA budget cuts. *Apollo's* demise was directly related to economic, philosophical, and political issues. Liberals believed congressional expenditures should be diverted from lunar exploration to address social ills. New York Congressman Ed Koch echoed the sentiments of many fellow lawmakers: "I just can't for the life of me see voting to find out whether there is some microbe on Mars, when in fact I know there are rats...in Harlem apartments."

At the same time, many Conservatives championed fiscal restraint and a shift from the big-government, *Great Society* mentality of the 1960s. Supporters of the burgeoning *environmentalist movement* also chimed in, alleging that the by-products of science and technology were destructive to the ecosystem.

The general public's long-standing fascination with lunar missions waned near the end of the *Apollo* program. After *CBS* preempted a popular prime time series to televise the *Apollo 17* launch, the network was inundated with complaints from angry viewers.

When *Project Apollo* was cancelled, the United States had not yet fully extracted itself from the costly and futile war in Vietnam. With so many competing agendas, space dollars became scarcer. In 1965, NASA's annual budget had been 5.25 billion dollars; by 1972, funding for the space program had shrunk to 3.3 billion dollars.

After scrubbing the final three *Apollo* lunar missions, the Nixon Administration devoted the lion's share of space appropriations to the Space Transportation System (STS), which would later become known as the Space Shuttle. *Apollo 17* astronaut Eugene Cernan remains the last man to have walked on the Moon. In 1976, the Soviet Union's *Luna 24* became the last unmanned vehicle to land on the Moon in the 20th century.

In the 40 plus years since the *Apollo 11* mission, the United States, Soviet Union, Japan, India, and the European Space Agency have continued to launch unmanned spacecraft into lunar orbit. In 1994, an American space probe, *Clementine*, orbited the Moon and generated the first global lunar topographical map.

In 1998, another American spacecraft, the *Lunar Prospector*, began orbiting the Moon with highly sophisticated molecular detection equipment. Utilizing neutron spectrometry, the unmanned probe discovered excess hydrogen in the Moon's Polar

Regions—suggesting the possibility of hidden water stores on the lunar surface.

On June 18, 2009, the 79 million-dollar Lunar Crater Observation Sensing Satellite (LCROSS) was launched from Cape Canaveral, entering into lunar orbit, 31 miles above the Moon's pock-marked surface. On October 10th of that same year, the *Centaur* portion of the spacecraft (roughly the size of a sports utility vehicle) separated from its *Atlas V* rocket, and crashed into the Moon's surface at the *Cabeus* crater. Traveling at a velocity of 5,600 miles per hour, the spacecraft generated a hole, 100 feet in diameter, at impact. The resulting dust cloud rose six miles into the lunar sky, allowing the LCROSS to analyze its contents. The plume's content included 220 pounds of ice, equivalent to 26 gallons of water.

"We always think of the Moon as dead, and this is sort of a dynamic process going on," University of Maryland astronomer Jessica Sunshine enthusiastically reported.

Further exploration by India's *Chandrayaan-1* lunar orbiter detected an estimated 600 million tons of frozen water in vast reservoirs at the bottom of craters near the Moon's North Pole. The ice deposits, permanently shaded from sunlight, are estimated to contain 100 times more water than previously thought. The stores of frozen water, two and one-half times the volume of the Great Lakes, are large enough to cover the entire lunar surface in a three-feet-deep sea.

The existence of water on the Moon bodes well for future lunar exploration and colonization. According to NASA geologist, Paul Spudis, lunar water can be purified for drinking purposes and also used to generate oxygen: "Now we can say, with a fair degree of confidence, that a sustainable human presence on the Moon is possible."

Many space enthusiasts long for establishment of a permanent lunar space colony. Moon colony supporters cite the need for a lunar launch pad, which could be used to fire missiles at asteroids and comets threatening to collide with Earth, and also provide mankind a safe haven in the event of Armageddon. Unless more compelling and less far-fetched arguments are offered, the prospect of lunar colonization will be a tough sell to American tax payers.

Nonetheless, many Americans still dream of one day returning to the Moon. On October 28, 2009, a prototype of NASA's 21st century lunar launch rocket blasted-off from Cape Canaveral. The successful launch of the 327-feet-tall, 425 million-dollar *Ares-I-X* was part of *Project Constellation;* an ambitious plan to transport the *Orion* crew capsule on manned missions to the Moon, Mars, and possibly other planets.

America's hopes for future manned lunar exploration were dealt a powerful setback on February 1, 2010, when President Barack Obama announced the cancellation of *Project Constellation.* The 100 billion-dollar funding for lunar exploration was instead diverted to future NASA rocketry development.

At the end of the space shuttle program in 2011, the United States became dependent on Russian Soyuz rockets to ferry American space crews to and from the International Space Station (ISS), for at least seven years. The United States will reimburse Russia 51 million dollars for each astronaut launched into space; considerably more than the 35 million dollars Russia charges private citizens. As of 2012, Russia undertakes 40 percent of all global space launches.

The demise of the space shuttle was predicted to send economic shock waves throughout the Cape Canaveral area. In early 2010, Florida's Brevard County anticipated a loss of 23,000 jobs after the shuttle stopped flying; 9,000 *direct* jobs at the Kennedy Space Center, and 14,000 *indirect* jobs in retail businesses, hotels, and restaurants.

What is America's future for manned space exploration? In September of 2011, NASA unveiled its 30-story Space Launch System, which will be powerful enough to take astronauts to the Moon and beyond. The 18 billion-dollar rocket, featuring five space shuttle main engines augmented by strap-on boosters, is designed to lift 77 tons of cargo into space. The rocket will carry a modified version of the *Orion* space capsule, originally designed for the defunct *Constellation* program.

NASA plans to launch an unmanned Space Launch System rocket in 2017. If this flight proves successful, a manned launch is thought to be feasible by 2021.

In the four plus decades since the conclusion of *Project Apollo,* the American space program has largely shifted its focus away from the Moon. At the same time, the much ballyhooed Space Race has been supplanted by a cooperative spirit. In May of 1972, President Richard Nixon and Soviet Premier Aleksei Kosygin signed a five-year *Agreement Concerning Cooperation in the Exploration and Use of Outer Space for Peaceful Purposes.* On July 17, 1975, an American *Apollo* capsule and a Soviet *Soyuz* spacecraft docked in Earth's orbit. The American and Russian crews exchanged handshakes and gifts, and also practiced joint docking maneuvers. The joint space mission marked a rare warming of Cold War tensions between the former Space Race competitors.

"How this new era will go depends on the determination, commitment, and faith of both our countries, and the world," *Apollo-Soyuz* mission commander Tom Stafford proudly proclaimed.

In May of 1973, the last NASA *Saturn V* rocket to lift-off in the 20th century launched *Skylab*—the world's first orbiting space station. *Skylab* was equipped with enough oxygen, water, and food to allow astronaut crews to remain in space for several weeks at a time. As large as a three-bedroom house, with 13,000 cubic feet of space, *Skylab* offered unprecedented space flight luxuries, including ovens, hot plates, showers, sinks, toilets, and a stationary bicycle. The astronauts visiting the space station were able to wear regular clothes, and were only required to don their bulky spacesuits during launch, re-entry, and extravehicular excursions.

Skylab crews conducted a variety of zero gravity experiments on fish, mice, and spiders. On-board telescopes allowed observers to gain a clearer view of the solar system, and enabled them to take detailed photographs of the Sun. The last *Skylab* crew established a new record—84 consecutive days in space.

Skylab was abandoned in 1974, with plans to bring it out of its dormant state, once the space shuttle program was underway. After an unanticipated deterioration of battery power, the space station began experiencing orbital decay in 1977. On July 11, 1979, during its fiery re-entry into Earth's atmosphere, *Skylab* fell in pieces over the Indian Ocean and Western Australia.

Post-Apollo, NASA's exploration of distant planets steadily increased. In December of 1973, *Pioneer 10* provided NASA with its first close-up photographs of Jupiter. On March 29, 1974, *Mariner 10* became the first space probe to orbit Mercury and send back detailed images of the planet closest to the Sun. On July 20, 1976, exactly seven years after the *Apollo 11* Moon landing, NASA landed a probe on Mars, marking the first successful exploration of another planet. In September of that same year, *Viking 2* also landed on the Red Planet. Since that time, numerous unmanned space probes have traveled to other planets, providing detailed information about orbital, environmental, and topographical characteristics of those extraterrestrial bodies.

In August of 2012, NASA achieved a milestone in planetary exploration, when the 2.5 billion-dollar *Curiosity* rover successfully landed in Mars' 3.5 billion-year-old *Gale Crater.* The landing of the rover, which descended into the thin Martian atmosphere at 13,200 miles per hour, was a complex maneuver. After being slowed by a giant parachute, *Curiosity* was lowered to Mars' surface by a specially-designed "sky crane."

The nuclear-powered, one-ton rover (the size of an automobile) is scheduled to spend two years (and perhaps longer) exploring Mars. The vehicle will ascend *Aeolis Mons* (*Mount Sharp*), a three-mile-high mountain, enabling NASA scientists to gain a better understanding of the Red Planet's geological history and provide clues as to whether the Martian environment is capable of supporting life. The rover is equipped with cameras and instrumentation to test rock and soil samples. Among *Curiosity's* most innovative features is a rock-vaporizing laser; once the solid rocks are transformed into gas, instruments aboard the rover can identify the specimen's chemical make-up. Data from *Curiosity* will be transmitted to the *Odyssey* satellite orbiting Mars, and then relayed back to Earth.

Attempts to visit Mars have been fraught with challenges. As of August of 2012, 41 probes have been launched by various world space agencies. In 26 cases, the missions have failed due to probes exploding in Earth's atmosphere, straying off course, losing power in transit, crashing onto the Martian surface, or failing to operate after a successful landing.

Launched on September 5, 1977, *Voyager 1* has maintained steady progress toward visiting distant galaxies. As of June 2012, the space probe was 11 billion miles from Earth, approaching *heliopause;* the point where solar winds stop, and magnetic fields shift from the solar system to deep space. Travelling at the speed of light, microwave radio signals take 16.7 hours to travel from *Voyager* to Earth. At some point, between 2012 and 2014, *Voyager 1* will become the first spacecraft to leave the solar system. As it races through interstellar space, sometime between 2020 and 2025, the probe will gradually lose power and be unable to transmit further scientific data back to Earth.

NASA's space shuttle program took flight in 1981. For the first time in manned space exploration history, a reusable, rocket-launched spacecraft was engineered to fly back to Earth and land on a runway. To provide additional thrust, shuttles were equipped with two strap-on solid rocket boosters, as well as a large external fuel tank. The 154-feet-long tank contained 385,000 gallons of liquid hydrogen and 140,000 gallons of liquid oxygen, which fueled the spacecraft's three internal engines. The solid rocket boosters were designed to be jettisoned two minutes after lift-off and parachuted into the Atlantic Ocean, where they would be retrieved and refurbished for future flights. Eight minutes after launch, the external fuel tank would be jettisoned, burning up during re-entry. The less costly external fuel tank design was criticized by some engineers as too risky, foretelling future catastrophe.

The inaugural space shuttle mission occurred on April 12, 1981, when *Columbia,* piloted by astronauts Robert L. Crippen and John Young (a veteran *Apollo* Moon walker), was launched from Cape Canaveral. Circling Earth 36 times over the course of two days, the mission was deemed a success. Though overlooked as a minor problem at the time, NASA engineers noted that 16 of the shuttle's outer protective tiles had been lost during lift-off (another 148 were damaged).

The space shuttle, much larger than previous spacecraft, was designed to accommodate a nine-person crew, and capable of carrying much larger payloads, including full-sized satellites. In addition to astronauts, space shuttle crews included *mission* and *payload specialists,* including scientists, teachers, and technicians.

On June 18, 1983, Sally Ride became the first American woman to fly in space, serving as a mission specialist aboard *Challenger.* On launch day, enthusiastic spectators, celebrating another milestone in equal rights, waved signs: RIDE, SALLY RIDE. Since that time, a number of other women have ventured into space. On October 11, 1984, Kathy Sullivan became the first American woman to walk in space.

While the early years of the shuttle program proved highly successful, the often-overlooked, but dangerous realities of space exploration were cruelly exposed on January 28, 1986, when *Challenger* exploded, 73 seconds after launch. A rubber O-ring on the right solid rocket booster, which had been hardened by unseasonably cold Florida weather, ruptured during lift-off, causing the booster to leak flames during the shuttle's ascent. At an altitude of 48,000 feet, the malfunctioning booster came completely loose and slammed into the external fuel tank, igniting 300,000 gallons of liquid hydrogen and 100,000 gallons of liquid oxygen. The force of the explosion, which the astronauts may well have survived, propelled the crew compartment 17,000 feet higher. Free falling from an altitude of 65,000 feet, the still-intact portion of the shuttle struck the Atlantic Ocean at a velocity of 207 miles per hour, which would have most certainly killed the crew; even if they had survived the fuel tank explosion.

Following the *Challenger* disaster, the entire space shuttle fleet was grounded for 32 months. During this hiatus, changes in shuttle design were affected and new safety measures were adopted. The updated space shuttle took flight again in 1988, highlighted by 77-year-old Ohio Senator John Glenn's return to space, 36 years after he became the first American to orbit the Earth.

On February 1, 2003, another grim reminder of the hazards of space travel unfolded over the skies of Texas and Louisiana. The space shuttle *Columbia* broke into pieces during the re-entry process, killing its seven-member crew. The cause of the tragedy was attributed to the long-identified, but largely ignored problem of protective tile loss and damage during launch. Further safety revisions followed, and the space shuttle remained America's lone manned spacecraft until its retirement in 2011.

On February 24, 2011, *Discovery* lifted off from Cape Canaveral's launch pad 39-A, marking its 39th and final flight into space. The space shuttle transported an American-built space station module, spare parts, a robot, and six-person crew to the International Space Station (ISS). When *Discovery* docked at the space station alongside a Russian *Soyuz* spacecraft and unmanned spaceships from Europe and Japan, it marked the first time in history that vehicles from every country capable of traveling to and from space were parked side-by-side. On March 9th, *Discovery* returned to Earth for the final time. Having flown for 27 years, *Discovery* spent a total of 365 days in space, traveled 148,000,000 miles, and orbited Earth 5,830 times.

In July of 2011, *Atlantis* landed at the Kennedy Space Center in Cape Canaveral, formally ending the 30-year space shuttle program. Over the course of the shuttle's lengthy history, nearly 15,000 people worked on the project.

Discovery will spend its retirement years at the *Steven F. Udvar-Hazy Center* at Washington D.C.'s Dulles Airport, as one of the exhibits featured at the Smithsonian Institute's National Air and Space Museum. The test shuttle *Enterprise* will be displayed at the *Intrepid Sea, Air, and Space Museum* in New York City. *Atlantis* will remain at Cape Canaveral's *Kennedy Space Center* Visitor Center, while *Endeavor* will reside at the *California Science Center* in Los Angeles.

In the late 1990s, construction was begun on the International Space Station (ISS); a joint venture between the United States, Soviet Union, Canada, Japan, and the 17-country European Space Agency. A Russian service module serves as the control center and living quarters for crews aboard the ISS, and is connected to a separate orbital laboratory. Upon completion, the interior of the ISS will be as large as a *Boeing 747* jet airliner. Solar panels generate energy for the space station, and a large robotic arm is utilized for payload transfers and construction work. The 100 billion-dollar ISS remains under active construction and renovation. Crews remain in orbit for five months, until a new group arrives, allowing the ISS to maintain continuous operation. A Russian *Soyuz* spacecraft remains docked at the orbital station to serve as a "life boat" in the event of an emergency.

On March 13, 2009, ISS crew members were forced to seek shelter in the *Soyuz* spacecraft, when orbiting debris (pieces of on old rocket) threatened to strike the space station. Fortunately, the *space junk*, traveling 17,500 miles per hour, missed the ISS. Had the debris collided with one of the space station's pressurized modules, the crew would have been left with only 10 minutes of oxygen, forcing them to return to Earth.

By today's estimates, some 500 pieces of debris orbit the Earth. NASA currently utilizes radar maps that can pinpoint orbiting objects as small as five centimeters, hoping to avert potentially catastrophic collisions.

In the 1990s, the *Hubble* space telescope was launched into orbit from the payload section of a space shuttle. Three years later, a shuttle crew repaired the telescope's focusing mechanism, which dramatically improved image quality. Orbiting 375 miles above Earth, *Hubble* has enabled observers to view 40 billion new galaxies and observe a *black hole* for the first time. Without having to penetrate the haze of Earth's atmosphere, the tractor trailer truck-sized telescope can magnify distant objects more clearly than any land-based instrument. The *Hubble* telescope operates in conjunction with the European Space Agency, and is radio controlled from the Goddard Space Flight Center in Greenbelt, Maryland.

The *James Webb* space telescope is scheduled to be launched no later than 2018. Twenty-one feet-wide and 100 times more powerful than *Hubble,* the *Webb* telescope is projected to cost 6.8 billion dollars by the time it is fully constructed.

The United States and Russia remain parties to the *Outer Space Treaty.* The pact specifies that no country can claim ownership of the Moon, which is under the same jurisdiction as international waters. The treaty also restricts the use of the Moon for peaceful purposes, banning the installation of military stations and weapons of mass destruction.

In April of 2001, American businessman Dennis Tito paid 20 million dollars to fly to the International Space Station aboard a Russian *Soyuz* spacecraft, inaugurating the private-sector's involvement in space exploration. On June 21, 2004, *Space Ship One,* piloted by Mike Melvill, became the first private vehicle to carry a human into space. Private funding will be an essential component of future space exploration, but space enthusiasts worry that free market investors will be unwilling to spend the billions of dollars needed each year necessary to match NASA's level of investment. Private-sector critics are also concerned about the safety and reliability of rockets and spacecraft designed without NASA's supervision.

While seeking active collaboration with the private-sector, NASA has established strict guidelines for space exploration. To preserve historical integrity, the space agency has warned future lunar explorers not to disrupt the relics from the six *Apollo* Moon-landing missions.

On May 22, 2012, the California-based company *SpaceX* utilized its *Falcon 9* rocket to launch an unmanned *Dragon* capsule into orbit. The 180-feet tall rocket, weighing over 700,000 pounds and powered by nine *Merlin 1C* engines, performed flawlessly; and, for the first time in history, a private-sector company spacecraft rendezvoused with the International Space Station. After the *Dragon* docked with the ISS, the six astronauts aboard the space station unloaded 1,000 pounds of cargo from the visiting space-craft, including food, clothing, batteries, a lap top computer, and 15 student-designed experiments. After nearly a week in space, the *Dragon* capsule returned to Earth with 1,455 pounds of cargo collected from the ISS (including personal items, old equipment, and completed experiments), splashing down in the Pacific Ocean.

During its maiden flight, *Falcon 9's* second stage rocket carried the ashes of 308 people, including actor James Doohan, who was among the cast members of the popular *Star Trek* television series, and *Mercury/Gemini* astronaut Gordon Cooper. The distribution of the ashes stored in the jettisoned rocket stage was a collaborative project between *SpaceX* and *Celestis,* a memorial space flight company.

In June of 2012, NASA Administrator Charles Bolden met with *SpaceX* officials at the company's McGregor, Texas facility to officially accept the cargo package *Dragon* had transported home from the ISS. The well-publicized meeting cemented the bond between the private-sector and America's legendary space agency.

The *Dragon* mission was part of NASA's Commercial Orbital Transportation Services Program, a private-sector cargo-delivery service designed to replace the retired space shuttle. The program is part of NASA's plan to out-source orbital missions, such that the space agency can focus on development of new spacecraft and rockets for more distant missions to the Moon and planets.

SpaceX, founded in 2002 by billionaire Elon Musk, has entered into a 1.6 billion-dollar contract to fly at least 12 unmanned missions to the International Space Station between 2012 and 2015. *SpaceX* is scheduled to launch its second cargo-laden spacecraft to the ISS in early October of 2012. The *Dragon* capsule, featuring wing-like, deployable solar panels, is scheduled for future modification, allowing the spacecraft to transport a seven-passenger crew.

Orbital Sciences Corporation, based out of Dulles, Virginia, is among three other companies that have contracted with NASA to develop spacecraft capable of transporting cargo and astronauts to the ISS. The company is planning the first test flight of its *Cygnus* spacecraft and *Antares* rocket in 2012.

Virgin Galactic, headed by its flamboyant CEO Richard Branson, has already signed up more than 500 passengers to fly aboard *Spaceship Two,* which will be designed to transport six people at a time to an altitude of 62 miles. At an individual cost of $200,000.00, space passengers will be able to view the curvature of the Earth, as well as unbuckle their seatbelts for a few minutes, in order to experience the sensation of weightlessness. While the 2012 target date for its maiden voyage proved too ambitious, *Virgin Galactic* remains committed to offering commercial space flights. The project has been plagued by misfortune; in 2007, during a test of *Spaceship Two,* a fuel tank explosion killed three engineers. In addition, construction of the company's New Mexico-based *Spaceport America* has been slowed by contractor disputes.

Armadillo Aerospace and *XCOR Aerospace* have also announced plans to develop and launch spacecraft for commercial passengers. Meanwhile, Russia has formulated plans for a space hotel, known as the Commercial Space Station. Orbiting 250 miles-high, at a velocity of 18,600 miles per hour, the hotel will allow tourists to remain in space from three days up to six months.

Space tourism will not be for the faint of heart. The chance of rocket failure during a space launch is estimated to be 1 in 20, contrasted with the 1 in 5,000,000 odds of a passenger dying on a commercial airliner.

The American military continues to maintain a presence in space, most noticeably with its reconnaissance satellites. In April of 2010, the Air Force launched its unmanned *OTV-1 (Orbital Test Vehicle 1)* spacecraft, which spent 225 days in orbit on a classified mission, before returning to Earth in December of that year. On March 5, 2011, the Air Force launched the *X-37B* (also known as the *OTV-2)* robotic spacecraft. Similar in design to the space shuttle, but considerably smaller (29-feet-long and 15-feet-wide), the *X-37B* is powered by an array of solar panels housed in its payload bed. The space plane's mission and payload are classified, but are believed to involve testing of spyware on Middle Eastern countries, specifically Afghanistan. Following an orbital path from 43 degrees north latitude to 43 degrees south latitude, the military spacecraft is well-positioned to keep a watchful eye on activities in this volatile region of the world. The *X-37B* is scheduled to return to Earth sometime in 2012.

As of 2102, NASA is focusing on development of launch rockets and spacecraft that will support long-distance manned space explorations. The space agency hopes to launch a manned mission to Mars during the 2030s. Such a mission will be a marathon endeavor; six to eight person-crews will spend six months reaching the Red Planet, remain on the Martian surface for 18 months, before returning to Earth.

Accordingly, space agency researchers are laboring to improve the taste and freshness of the food stores that will nourish the astronauts during long-distance missions. Present day ISS crewmembers can select from nearly 100 food options, all of which are freeze-dried, and have a shelf life of approximately two years. Weightlessness impairs both taste and smell, which has contributed to long-standing complaints about unsavory space food. In all likelihood, long-distance rations will be vegetarian, given the impracticality of preserving meat and dairy products. Future astronauts may well have the capability of preparing meals using pressure cookers. Researchers are also studying the feasibility of constructing hydroponic greenhouses, allowing space travelers to cultivate fresh vegetables and fruits.

In 1970, the crew of *Apollo 11* co-authored a book entitled, *First on the Moon*. Neil Armstrong, Buzz Aldrin, and Michael Collins soon went their separate ways, reuniting only for anniversaries of the historic lunar landing.

Shortly after completion of the *Apollo 11* mission, Neil Armstrong decided to end his space flight career. For 13 months, he served at the Pentagon as Deputy Associate Director for NASA's Office of Advanced Research and Technology. In 1971, Armstrong left the space program to pursue an academic career, and was appointed Professor of aerospace engineering and applied mechanics at the University of Cincinnati. While Armstrong technically held only honorary doctorates, students nonetheless addressed him as "Professor" or "Doctor." The former *Apollo 11* commander developed a pair of new courses for the engineering curriculum (*Aircraft Design* and *Experimental Flight Mechanics*), while hoping to maintain a life of relative anonymity: "I just wanted to be a University Professor and be permitted to do my research."

Armstrong was never a total recluse. In 1979, he became a national spokesperson for *Chrysler* Corporation, appearing in television and print advertisements. He also appeared as a paid endorser for *General Tire* and *Banker's Association of America,* as well as joining the boards of directors of several companies, including *Marathon Oil, United Airlines,* and *Thiokol.* Before retiring in 2002, Armstrong served as chairman of the board for *EDO Corporation.*

As a retired astronaut, Armstrong maintained a link with the space program. After the near-catastrophic explosion aboard *Apollo 13,* Armstrong served as a member of the investigatory committee reviewing the mishap. In 1986, he was appointed to the *Rogers Committee* investigating the fatal explosion of the space shuttle *Challenger.*

Armstrong was party to controversy surrounding his historic voyage to the Moon. Beginning in 1994, he largely refused to sign autographs, after learning that recipients were selling his signature for profit. That same year, Armstrong sued *Hallmark Cards* for unauthorized use of his "One small step for mankind" quote on a Christmas ornament. The lawsuit settled out of court, and Armstrong donated the award to his alma mater, Purdue University.

In 2005, Armstrong threatened legal action when his barber of 20 years, Max Sizemore, sold the former astronaut's hair clippings for $3,000.00, without first obtaining permission. When Sizemore was unable to retrieve the hair clippings, the barber avoided going to court by donating his profits to a charity of Armstrong's choosing.

Neil Armstrong was the recipient of numerous awards and honors, including the *Sylvanus Thayer Award* (presented by the

U.S. Military Academy at West Point for service to his country), the *Presidential Medal of Freedom,* the *Congressional Space Medal of Honor,* the *Congressional Gold Medal,* and the *Collier Trophy* (awarded by National Aeronautics Association). A handful of elementary, middle, and high schools now bear his name. The engineering building at Purdue University was named the *Neil Armstrong Hall of Engineering.* His hometown of Wapakoneta, Ohio, became home to the *Neil Armstrong Air and Space Museum.* The airport in New Knoxville, Ohio, where Armstrong took his first flying lessons, was renamed in his honor.

Armstrong remained active in aviation, piloting over 200 different types of aircraft during his storied career, including jets, propeller driven airplanes, rockets, helicopters, and gliders. In 1989, he was invited to fly the newly developed *B-1* bomber.

In his later years, Armstrong grew troubled over America's leadership role in space, particularly after NASA cancelled plans for a return mission to the Moon. Addressing a House of Representatives committee in 2010, the famed astronaut shared his concerns: "Some question why America should return to the Moon. After all, they say, 'We've been there.' I find that mystifying. It would be as if 16th century monarchs proclaimed that 'We need not go to the new world, we have already been there.'"

In February of 2012, Armstrong spoke at Ohio State University, during a ceremony honoring the 50th anniversary of John Glenn's inaugural orbit of Earth. Even though he was the official honoree, Glenn offered tribute to the *Apollo 11* commander: "To this day, he's the one person on Earth, I'm truly envious of." Three months later, Armstrong joined fellow retired astronaut Gene Cernan (the last man to walk on the Moon) at the opening of the National Flight Academy at the Naval Air Station in Pensacola, Florida. The aviation-oriented camp is designed to teach children about math and science—a project near and dear to Armstrong's heart.

In early August of 2012, Armstrong underwent surgery to bypass blockages in four of his coronary arteries. The former astronaut's health problems elicited an outpouring of affection. NASA Administrator Charles Bolden issued a formal statement on behalf of the space agency: "Neil's pioneering spirit will surely serve him well in this challenging time, and the entire NASA family is holding the Armstrong family in our thoughts and prayers. I know countless well-wishers around the world join us in sending get-well wishes to this true American hero." Armstrong's *Apollo 11* crewmate Buzz Aldrin wrote in his *Twitter* update: "Just heard about Neil and heart surgery today—sending my best wishes for a speedy recovery—we agreed to make it (to) the 50th *Apollo* anniversary in 2019."

Sadly, Armstrong developed serious post-operative complications and died on August 25, 2012, just 20 days after his 82nd birthday. Armstrong's death was followed by an outpouring of sympathy and acclaim.

"Neil was among the greatest of American heroes—not just of his time, but of all time. When he and his fellow crew members lifted off aboard *Apollo 11* in 1969, they carried with them the aspirations of an entire nation," President Barack Obama proclaimed.

Nancy Conrad, widow of *Apollo 12* commander Pete Conrad, remembered Armstrong fondly: "Neil was a humble and personable man…Although he was the first man to walk on the Moon, he never asserted his own ego into a conversation."

Buzz Aldrin shared remembrances of his *Apollo 11* crewmate: "I know I am joined by millions of others in mourning the passing of a true American hero, and the best pilot I ever knew. My friend Neil took the small step but giant leap that changed the world, and will forever be remembered as a landmark moment in human history." The third member of the *Apollo 11* mission, Michael Collins offered his condolences: "He was the best, and I will miss him terribly."

Armstrong never actively sought publicity for his role in history, and encouraged others to focus on the group effort that made lunar exploration a reality. In a 2005 interview, Armstrong candidly discussed the perils associated with the *Apollo 11* mission, estimating that the chances for a successful lunar landing were only about 50 percent: "I was elated, ecstatic and extremely surprised that we were successful."

Buzz Aldrin never returned to space after the *Apollo 11* Moon landing. In June of 1971, he left NASA after logging a total of 289 hours and 53 minutes in space. Aldrin has authored a handful of books, including *Return to Earth, Men from Earth, Magnificent Desolation,* and *Encounter with Tiber* (a science fiction novel). Aldrin has since worked as an aerospace consultant and motivational speaker. In 1992, he designed a computer strategy game, *Buzz Aldrin's Race into Space.*

Like his crewmate Neil Armstrong, Aldrin has encountered controversy related to his role in history. In September of 2002, Bart Sibrel, an investigative journalist who has loudly and repeatedly derided the *Apollo 11* mission as an elaborate hoax, confronted Aldrin outside a Beverly Hills Hotel; Sibrel had previously taunted Neil Armstrong in another public forum. Sibrel, the producer of a video entitled *A Funny Thing Happened on the Way to the Moon,* accosted Aldrin, with bible in hand, and accused him of being a "coward, liar, and thief." Unlike Armstrong, who had managed to ignore Sibrel's public tirade, Aldrin fought back. The 72-year-old astronaut, weighing only 160 pounds, punched his 37-year-old, 250-pound accuser in the face, knocking him to the ground. Sibrel filed a police report, but after reviewing videotape of the fracas, the Los Angeles County District Attorney declined to press charges.

In the early years after the first lunar landing, Aldrin lingered uneasily in the shadow of Neil Armstrong. *Apollo 11* crewmate Michael Collins commented on Aldrin's self-imposed dilemma: "Fame has not worn well on Buzz. I think he resents not being the first man on the Moon more than he appreciates being second." Aldrin has candidly discussed post-*Apollo 11* struggles: "The transition from 'astronaut preparing to accomplish the next big thing, to astronaut telling the last big thing,' did not come easily to me."

"I moved from drinking to depression to heavier drinking to deeper depression," Aldrin recalled.

Aldrin eventually achieved sobriety and became an active member of *Alcoholics Anonymous,* as well as a staunch advocate for the treatment of mental illness. Aldrin's personal struggles were dramatized in the 1976 television movie, *Return to Earth;* actor Cliff Robertson portrayed the famed astronaut.

Aldrin is a dedicated advocate of private-sector space exploration and future manned missions to the Moon and Mars. He has proposed establishment of a Moon base and development of *Lunar Cyclers*—a series of vehicles continuously orbiting the Earth and Moon, which would be utilized for transportation of space crews and cargo. Aldrin, who has proposed construction of permanent colonies on the Moon and Mars, believes that a manned mission to Mars is feasible by July 20, 2019—the 50th anniversary of *Apollo 11's* lunar landing.

Time will tell if Aldrin's proposal for a "unified space vision" for the 21st century will come to fruition. A poll released in June of 2010 revealed that the American public, by a margin of 50 to 31 percent, favored less government focus on space exploration, in light of the country's troubled economy. The poll findings were consistent with the Obama Administration's decision to outsource a significant portion of future space research and development to the private-sector.

In spite of Aldrin's personal struggles and self-doubts, his historical legacy is firmly entrenched. A Moon crater near the *Apollo 11* landing site is named in his honor, along with *asteroid number 6470.* He has been awarded honorary degrees from six universities, and was the recipient of the *Presidential Medal of Freedom* and *Robert Collier Trophy.* In 2001, President George W. Bush appointed Aldrin to the Commission on the Future of the United States' Aerospace Industry.

Like his *Apollo 11* crewmates, Michael Collins never again flew in space after the inaugural lunar mission. He departed NASA in January of 1970, and was appointed Assistant Secretary of State for Public Affairs, a position he occupied for two years. He was later named Director of the Smithsonian Institute's National Air and Space Museum, and eventually became the Undersecretary for the Smithsonian Institute. By the time he retired from the Air Force in 1978, Collins had achieved the rank of Major General.

Collins has authored a handful of books, including *Carrying the Fire, Flying to the Moon and Other Strange Places, Liftoff,* and *Mission to Mars.* He is also an accomplished watercolor artist, having painted scenes of the Everglades, near his home, as well as portraits of various aircraft he has flown over the course of his distinguished career. Collins now often refuses to sign his art work, after learning profiteers were re-selling the autographed portraits at inflated prices.

By the end of 1994, Collins had accumulated 5,000 hours of flying time, including 266 hours in space. *Asteroid number 6471* bears Collins' name, and he has been awarded the *NASA Distinguished Service Medal,* the *Air Force Distinguished Flying Cross,* and the *Presidential Medal of Freedom.* Along with his *Apollo 11* crewmates, Neil Armstrong and Buzz Aldrin, Michael Collins was honored with a star on Hollywood's *Walk of Fame.*

Apollo 11 Flight Director, Gene Kranz, was named Deputy Director of NASA Mission Operations in 1974, followed by promotion to the full directorship in 1983. In December of 1993, during his final days at Mission Control, Kranz supervised the space shuttle crew that repaired the *Hubble* space telescope. Kranz retired from NASA in March of 1994.

In February of 1970, less than a year after the *Apollo 11* lunar landing, the prime architect of the American space program, Wernher von Braun, moved from Huntsville, Alabama to Washington D.C. to become the Deputy Associate Administrator of NASA. Von Braun soon discovered that he missed being part of hands-on rocket development: "I felt like a mushroom—they kept me in the dark; once in a while, the door would open for some fertilizer to be shoveled in, and then the door would shut again." Two years later, frustrated by the cancellation of the *Apollo* Project, diminished enthusiasm for a manned mission to Mars, and decreased funding for the space program, von Braun left NASA to become Vice-President of Engineering for the aerospace company, *Fairchild Industries.*

Wernher von Braun died of cancer on January 16, 1977, and was buried in Alexandria, Virginia. A lunar crater was named in his honor—a permanent tribute to the rocket scientist's essential role in the American space program. In his lifetime, von Braun was awarded 12 honorary Doctorate degrees, and was the founder of the Research Institute at the University of Alabama in Huntsville.

In spite of the remarkable feats of von Braun's rocket team, dark shadows have loomed over their careers. By the late 1960s and early 1970s, many influential Jewish leaders protested that the German rocket scientists should be punished as ex-Nazis, rather than lionized as innovators in rocket technology. In 1973, when most of the original German-born employees of NASA were let go as part of the post-*Apollo* reduction in work force, there was little sympathy among those who accused them of being unreformed anti-Semites.

Even the famed von Braun could not fully escape this controversy. In 1976, a year before the rocket scientist's death, influential friends and colleagues lobbied President Gerald Ford to award von Braun the *Presidential Medal of Freedom*. Ford declined to present the award, likely influenced by a memorandum prepared by his advisor, David Gergen: "Sorry, but I can't support the idea of giving (the) Medal of Freedom to (a) former Nazi whose V-2 was fired into over 3,000 British and Belgian cities. He has given valuable service to the U.S. since, but frankly, he has gotten as good as he has given."

In 1984, Arthur Rudolph, who served as the *Saturn V* Project Manager during the height of the Space Race, was identified as a *war criminal* by Nazi hunters. The U.S. Department of Justice re-examined Rudolph's government file, which was compiled at the time of his arrival from Germany in 1945. One of the file's incriminating documents described the German as "100 percent Nazi" and "a dangerous type." Rudolph was subsequently accused of "working thousands of slave laborers to death," as well as concealing his involvement in the crimes. To avoid prosecution, the 77-year-old retired rocket scientist agreed to renounce his American citizenship and return to Germany, where he remained until his death in 1995.

Believing the rocket scientist had been wrongly accused, Rudolph's defenders unsuccessfully lobbied for restoration of his citizenship.

The historic relics of the *Apollo 11* mission remain on permanent display. The quarantine trailer, flotation collar, and capsule righting spheres are housed at the *Udvar-Hazy Center Annex* near Dulles Airport in Washington D.C. The heat-scarred command module, *Columbia,* is on display at the Smithsonian Institute's National Air and Space Museum.

Today, approximately 750 pounds of Moon rock and soil, collected from six different lunar landing sites, are housed in locations throughout the world. Some of the lunar rock samples are older than any geological specimens discovered on Earth, suggesting meteoric origin. In recognition of its age, one lunar specimen bears the name *Genesis Rock.* Another lunar rock, first discovered at *Tranquility Base,* is named *Armalcolite,* in honor of the *Apollo 11* crew. In 1984, after thoroughly analyzing the accumulated lunar rock and soil samples, a study group issued a consensus report endorsing the *Giant Impact Theory* as the most likely explanation for the origin of the Moon.

For those skeptics who doubt that American astronauts actually landed on the Moon, photographic images taken by the Lunar Reconnaissance Orbiter offer an inarguable rebuttal. The photographs, taken in July of 2009, from an altitude of 13 to 15 miles, offer definitive proof of the *Apollo* Moon landings. Images of *Tranquility Base* clearly show the *Eagle's* descent engine on the lunar surface. The Lunar Reconnaissance Orbiter's principle investigator, Mark Robinson, enthusiastically described the photographs: "The *LROC* team anxiously awaited each image. We were very interested in getting our first peak at the lunar module descent stages just for thrill—and to see how well the cameras had come into focus. Indeed, the images are fantastic and so is the focus." Additional photographs were taken of the remaining *Apollo* landing sites. Discarded scientific instruments and the astronaut's footprints are clearly visible at the location of the *Apollo 14* landing.

Apollo 17's moon buggy and its tire tracks are visible in another series of photographs.

The Space Race is broadly defined as a 12-year competition between the United States and Soviet Union, beginning with the launch of *Sputnik* in October of 1957, and ending with the *Apollo 11* lunar landing in July of 1969. Incredible sums of money were spent on the space program during this epic contest between Capitalism and Communism. The *Apollo* program cost 25.4 billion dollars, and the price tag for *Apollo 11* alone, was 355 million dollars. In 1965 and 1966, the high water marks for NASA expenditures, approximately four cents out of every American tax dollar were spent on the space program. At the peak of America's quest to land a man on the Moon, space was Florida's third largest industry, behind tourism and citrus fruit. In the years since the conclusion of the Space Race, the true value of the costly space program has been vigorously debated. Was it an investment in mankind's future or an expensive war of image and innovation waged against the Soviet Union?

Without a doubt, politics played a prominent role in propagating space exploration. Skilled politicians, most notably John F. Kennedy and Lyndon B. Johnson, capitalized on their countrymen's fears of Soviet nuclear annihilation to push forth a bold and costly initiative to land a man on the Moon. While manned space flight was reflective of the American spirit of exploration and a source of national pride, critics often cite politics and money as the prime motivators. Space historian, Gerard J. Degroot, summed up the feelings of many skeptics: "...The decision was based not on science, but cold hard politics. McNamara (Secretary of Defense under Presidents Kennedy and Johnson) needed to save the aerospace industry. Johnson wanted to restore American prestige. Congress worried about losing influence in the third world. Senators wanted fat contracts for their states. Kennedy needed to rescue his image (in the wake of the Bay of Pigs fiasco). Everyone wanted to beat the Russians."

At the same time, the technological legacy of the space program is indisputable. Weather tracking satellites, global positioning devices, bar codes (which were used by NASA to track parts), cordless tools, satellite dishes, smoke detectors, newly developed synthetic materials (including epoxies, graphite, and the popular lubricant, *WD-40*), diabetic insulin pumps, improved water filtration systems, and faster, more powerful computers are among the progeny of the American space program.

It is difficult to overlook the psychological implications of *Apollo's* legacy. By the late 1960s, many Americans had grown disillusioned by seemingly endless domestic and international problems. When Neil Armstrong stepped on the Moon, for a brief moment, nearly every American felt enormous pride. Walter Cronkite, who repeatedly provided the nation with eyewitness accounts of the Space Race, perhaps summed it up best: "The 1960s, when we first launched humans into space and went to the Moon, were in other ways a drain on our spirit. The civil rights battles, the frightening divisiveness of the Vietnam War, the horrible assassinations—they drained the American spirit. It's no exaggeration to say the space program saved us."

After *Project Apollo,* space exploration no longer commanded the attention it enjoyed during the 1960s. Flights of the space shuttle, unmanned explorations of distant planets, and experiments undertaken on the International Space Station have been frequently buried in the back pages of contemporary newspapers. Routine television programming is no longer preempted by rocket launches or live broadcasts from space.

The novelty of space exploration is now overshadowed by a plethora of new technologies and distractions, including cable and satellite television, lightening fast computers, sophisticated electronic games, smart phones, and the Internet, to name a few. Except for rare occasions, like the terrorist attacks of September 11, 2001, Americans infrequently experience a sense of national unity.

In an age where the war against terror, political squabbles, and economic uncertainty dominate the headlines, it is comforting to revisit that Sunday in July of 1969, when the world celebrated the news: *The Eagle has landed.*

BIBLIOGRAPHY

Books:

Aldrin, Buzz. *Reaching for the Moon.* Collins, 2005.

Aldrin, Buzz. *Magnificent Desolation: The Long Journey Home from the Moon.* Harmony Books, 2009.

Aldrin, Edwin E., Jr. *Return to Earth.* Random House, 1973.

Anderson, Dale. *Landmark Events in American History: The First Moon Landing.* World Almanac Library, 2004.

Brinkley, Douglas. *Cronkite.* Harper Collins Publishers, 2012.

Burrows, William E. *The New Ocean: The Story of the First Space Age.* Random House, 1998.

Carpenter, Scott M. and L. Gordon Cooper, John H. Glenn, Virgil I. Grissom, Walter M. Schirra, Alan B. Shepard, and Donald K. Slayton. *We Seven.* Simon & Schuster, 1962.

Chaiken, Andrew. *A Man on the Moon.* Penguin Books, 1994.

Chaiken, Andrew. *Man on the Moon: Lunar Explorers.* Time-Life Books, 1999.

Collins, Michael. *Carrying the Fire: An Astronaut's Journeys.* Cooper Square Press, 1974.

Craddock, Robert. *Apollo 11.* Chronicle Books, 2003.

Cronkite, Walter. *A Reporter's Life.* Alfred A. Knopf, 1996.

Degroot, Gerard J. *Dark Side of the Moon: The Magnificent Madness of the American Lunar Quest.* New York University Press, 2006.

Dickson, Paul. *Sputnik: The Shock of the Century.* Walker, 2001.

Englehart, Steve. *Countdown to the Moon.* iUniverse.com, Inc., 1994.

Goodwin, Robert. *Apollo 11: First Men on the Moon.* Apogee Books, 1971.

Hansen, James R. *First Man: The Life of Neil A. Armstrong.* Simon & Schuster, 2005.

Hardesty, Von and Gene Eisman. *Epic Rivalry: The Inside Story of the Soviet and American Space Race.* National Geographic Society, 2007.

Kraft, Chris. *Flight: My Life in Mission Control.* Dutton, 2001.

Kranz, Gene. *Failure is not an Option: Mission Control from Mercury to Apollo 13 and Beyond.* Berkley Books, 2000.

Lamb M.D., Lawrence E. *Inside the Space Race: A Space Surgeon's Diary.* Synery Books, 2006.

Lawrence, Richard Russell. *The Mammoth Book of Space Exploration and Disasters.* Carol & Graf, 2005.

NASA archives. *Apollo 11: NASA Mission Reports, Volumes 1 and 2,* 1971.

Neufeld, Michael J. *Von Braun: Dreamer of Space, Engineer of War.* Knopf, 2007.

Slayton, Donald K. *Deke!* Forge, 1994.

Smith, Jeffrey K. *Bad Blood: Lyndon B. Johnson, Robert F. Kennedy, and the Tumultuous 1960s.* Authorhouse, 2010.

Swanson, Glen E., Ed. *Before This Decade: Personal Reflections on the Apollo Program.* University Press of Florida, 2002.

Thimmesh, Catherine. *Team Moon: How 400,000 People Landed Apollo 11 on the Moon.* Houghton-Mifflin Company, 2006.

Winterstein, Sr., William E. *Secrets of the Space Age.* Robert D. Reed Publishers, 2005.

Wolfe, Tom. *The Right Stuff.* Picador, 1979.

Web Resources:

www.history.nasa.gov
www.alert.org/thenews
www.thespaceplace.com
www.astronomytoday.com
www.nasm.si.edu
www.spaceflight.nasa.gov

www.solarviews.com
www.klabs.org/history
www.chron.com
www.parkes.atnf.csi.ro
www.archives.gov
www.science.ksc.gov
www.lunarhall.org
www.timesonline.co.uk
www.collectspace.com
www.news.nationalgeographic.com
www.cockpitvoicerecordings.com
www.apollo.sese.asu.edu
www.apollotv.net
www.adsabs.harvard.edu/abs
www.lunar.arc.nasa.gov
www.science.nasa.gov
www.aviationnow.com
www.moonphaseinfo.com
www.psrd.hawaill.edu
www.nineplanets.org
www.abcnews.com
www.cosmosmagazine.com
www.cnn.com
www.cincinnati.com
www.jsc.nasa.gov.
www.spaceflighthistory.com
www.buzzaldrin.com
www.time.com
www.redstone.army.mil
www.history.msfc.nasa.gov
www.earthobservatory.nasa.gov
www.v2rocket.com
www.nytimes.com
www.msnbc.com
www.theweek.com
www.breitbart.com

www.cbsnews.com
www.usaweekend.com
www.usatoday.com
www.ap.com
www.upi.com
www.floridatoday.com
www.space.com
www.scientificamerican.com
www.washingtonpost.com
www.cpf.cleanprint.net
www.latimes.com

ACKNOWLEDGEMENTS

In writing a narrative of the *Apollo 11* mission, the author utilized an abundance of material made available by NASA, as well as the research efforts of the numerous individuals listed in the Bibliography—I am most appreciative of their work. My narrative is by no means a definitive history of the American and Soviet space programs. Entire volumes have been devoted to various aspects of space exploration, along with lengthy biographies of many of the individuals mentioned in this chronicle. A significant portion of this book is *rocket science,* as written by a *non-rocket scientist,* so I can only hope I did not sacrifice complexity for the sake of conciseness.

Once again, my editor, Jim Fulmer, unselfishly gave of his time, helping me craft a readable book. This is our seventh book together, and I remain privileged to call him my friend.

My wife, Anne, patiently endured another book with me, offering her unwavering support and encouragement, while, once again, reviewing my manuscript. I love her very much.

My sons, Andy and Ben, are the lights in my life. I love them more than I can put into words.

It is my sincere hope you found *The Eagle Has Landed: The Story of the Apollo 11* both entertaining and informative. Thank you for taking time to read this book.

ABOUT THE AUTHOR

Jeffrey K. Smith is a physician and writer. A native of Enterprise, Alabama, he earned his undergraduate and medical degrees from the University of Alabama. After completing his residency at the William S. Hall Psychiatric Institute, Dr. Smith entered private practice in upstate South Carolina.

The author resides in Greer, South Carolina with his wife, Anne. They are the proud parents of two sons, Andy and Ben.

OTHER BOOKS BY
JEFFREY K. SMITH

Murder-Mystery Novels:

Sudden Despair

Two Down, Two to Go

A Phantom Killer

Non-fiction:

Rendezvous in Dallas: The Assassination of John F. Kennedy

The Fighting Little Judge: The Life and Times of George C. Wallace

Fire in the Sky: The Story of the Atomic Bomb

Bad Blood: Lyndon B. Johnson, Robert F. Kennedy, and the Tumultuous 1960s

Dixiecrat: The Life and Times of Strom Thurmond

The Loyalist: The Life and Times of Andrew Johnson

To learn more about these books, please visit: **www.newfrontier-publications.net**

CPSIA information can be obtained
at www.ICGtesting.com
Printed in the USA
FSHW022018061218
54305FS